636.7088

D0446527

The Road to

Westminster

How to Select and Train
a Purebred Dog and
Prepare It for the Show Ring

Robert B. Freeman
& Toni C. Freeman

BETTERWAY PUBLICATIONS, INC.
WHITE HALL, VIRGINIA

91492
AULT PUBLIC LIBRARY
AULT, COLORADO

Published by Betterway Publications, Inc.
P.O. Box 219
Crozet, VA 22932
(804) 823-5661

Cover design by Susan Reilly
Cover photograph by Helen Boyer
Photographs by Robert and Toni Freeman
Illustrations by Jennifer V. Wallace
Typography by Park Lane Associates

Copyright © 1990 by Robert B. Freeman and Toni C. Freeman

All rights reserved. No part of this book may be reproduced by any means, except by a reviewer who wishes to quote brief excerpts in connection with a review in a magazine or newspaper.

Library of Congress Cataloging-in-Publication Data

Freeman, Robert B., 1938-
    The road to Westminster : selecting and training a purebred dog
and preparing it for the show ring / by Robert B. Freeman and Toni
C. Freeman.
        p. cm.
    Includes index.
    ISBN 1-55870-169-9 (v. 1) : $8.95
    1. Dogs--Showing. 2. Dog shows. I. Freeman, Toni C. 1946-
II. Title.
SF425.F74 1990
636.7′088′8--dc20   90-39082
                                                                CIP

Printed in the United States of America
0 9 8 7 6 5 4 3 2 1

In Loving Memory
of
Coventry's Danny Boy

Portrait by Jack Helman

Never a blue ribbon or a trophy, but Danny won the hearts of all who knew him. Nursemaid to puppies, the clown who made us laugh, the very best kitty washer in history, our dearest friend. We can only hope they give lots of cookies in heaven.

Acknowledgments

We wish to express gratitude to the following for their contributions to this volume:

All Clumber Spaniels who ever lived
Every other breed of dog, past and present
Ron and Louise Larsen, breeders of our first Clumber
Bill and Sandy Blakeley, our mentors
James A. Boatman, V.M.D., for many years of compassionate
    animal care
The Altoona Area Kennel Club, for continuing support
James W. Takacs, V.M.D., reviewer of all things medical
The Weekend Warriors, from whom we continue to learn
The Judges and A.K.C., without whom and which we would have
    to blame ourselves
Kathy Zalewski, our borrowed handler, helper, kid

Preface

To all individuals and families seeking a wholesome recreation, we extend an invitation to join us in the wonderful world of Dog Shows. The sport of showing dogs provides opportunities for travel and competition, and for making friends from all walks of life. If those enticements are not enough to prompt an investigation, try this. The sport of showing dogs affords you an opportunity to share and bond with a purebred animal who will love you, unconditionally, for as long as he lives. We suggest that you will have to look long and far to beat that package of benefits.

Please do not misunderstand. Our invitation does not entitle you to ruby shoes and a yellow brick road. As with any sport worth pursuing, this one has methods and rules. Learn and practice and learn more. With patience, you and your dog could one day stand in the spotlight at Westminster. And even if your animal never quite makes superstar, you, the dog, and everyone else on the team will enjoy each other and the effort.

To better your chances for success, we offer you *The Road to Westminster*. This volume, and Volume II, to follow, are designed to guide you through the mists and confusions. Every year many leave the sport for the want of a little help and direction. The loss of those potential assets, canine and human, saddens us and most of the other veterans. It is our sincere hope that these volumes provide you with that help and direction and that we shall see you in that ring.

Bob and Toni Freeman

Contents

I

Getting Involved

1.

The Doggy Balance Sheet

"Does it balance for us?"

To be competitive, a golfer needs clubs; a tennis player, a racquet; and a dog, his handler. That's right! The animal is the contestant. You and your team only share his accomplishments. Legally, you own the dog. In actuality, quite the reverse appears true.

Before jumping in, ask yourself if you feel ready to be owned by a dog. Do not rush your answer. Come with us while we investigate together some of the preparations required. Puppy-proofing the facility, we call it. The cost and energy expenditure may be more than you guessed. Once you know the facts, we will be happy to listen to your answer.

FENCING THE YARD

"Should we have a fenced yard?"

We realize that a fenced yard may be an impossibility for apartment dwellers and many who do not own the property on which they live. You could do what we did, buy a house and move. But even that may not solve the problem. Before prospective and current property owners rush off and spend their money, they should check the ordinances and restrictive covenants in their community. In some communities, ordinances prohibit fencing of any kind, or they dictate what type of fencing you may use. Those of you who have the option of fencing and can afford it should do so. The obvious benefit of a fenced yard is that it confines your dog, while it keeps other people and dogs out.

Your animal will need exercise, perhaps as much as two miles a day. Even if you enjoy exercise, what happens on those busy, inclement, sick, or lazy days when you cannot hook on the lead and take Throckmorton for this two mile jaunt? You can open the door and invite Throck into his fenced yard, or fenced run, where he can exercise himself. Think, too, about those rainy six o'clock mornings and snowy eleven o'clock evenings. What a wonderful time to let him out unescorted to perform his eliminations!

Remember that you must assume liability for Throck. When someone wanders into your yard, fenced or unfenced, and Throck proves his teeth can puncture, you better have insurance. As well fenced as our property is, we still carry a rider on our homeowner's insurance against such eventualities. And have you ever heard of dog-nappers? They do exist and they steal dogs to sell them to laboratories for experimentation and research.

You say you are thinking more of a Throckmortana than a Throckmorton. No objection here, but when she goes into heat, you will wish that you had fenced your yard, or chosen the Throckmorton.

Finally, consider your neighbors. The next time you mow your lawn and step in your neighbor's dog's droppings, or your neighbor's dog's visit awakens you at three in the morning, answer for yourself why strong fences make good neighbors.

"What kind of fence should we use?"

Without hesitation, your first choice should be chain link, nine gauge, six feet high. "Six feet high?" We hear the whispers questioning our sanity. "But he is a little skunk of a dog," you say. "He couldn't clear four feet if his life depended on it." Maybe Throck is limited, but humans and bigger dogs are not. We have two German Shepherds that could clear your four foot fence without missing a stride.

Chain link costs more than some of the other choices on the market, but it will last indefinitely. And your animal will not try very hard or long to chew through it. Unless you live on a really tight budget, let the company you buy from install the fence. They have the tools and the know-how, or they should. If you plan to spend the rest of your life where you live now, have them cement in the vertical poles, with the top of the cement at least a foot under the ground. With the concrete that far underground, Throck will not try to dig under the block and wind up with scars all over his nose. Or if you question how long you might live at your present location, you can have them use anchors in place of concrete and then dig them up when you move.

If you number among the ambitious and have a strong back, you might want to dig a ditch four to six inches deep, along the line where you intend the fence to stand, and have the installer set the fence in the ditch. Rocks and roots can make the digging a disagreeable task, but the ditch will discourage Throck from trying to dig under. With many breeds, such as terriers, for instance, digging and its prevention warrant serious thought. The ditch will also add rigidity to the bottom of the fence and save the cost of bottom rails.

You may consider the cost of chain link prohibitive. It is certainly not cheap, but the price of stockade fence will not excite you either. Stockade provides an alternative, but, in our opinion, not a good one. It deteriorates with age, the ugly side faces your yard, and most dogs will chew at it. Not nibble, chew! And once Throck discovers he can chew, he will aspire to ever-greater accomplishments. Also, stockade fencing establishes a solid barrier and for some reason, this type of enclosure seems to raise the hostility level of neighbors. They eventually hold your dog responsible for the fence.

Perhaps the best alternative to chain link, depending on Throck's size and strength of jaw, is a rail fence, with wire mesh attached to the inside. Buy the sturdiest wire you can find, with openings no larger than two by four inches. Use the heavy duty, hard to pound, rounded staples to secure the fence to the rails.

Caution! Either of our Shepherds or Clumbers could chew through wire fencing in no time. As a matter of fact, we have some wire fencing from an emergency facility we once constructed, with Shepherd size holes in it, which we can sell cheap to the first caller. Once the animal knows he can get through, replacing the damaged wire with new sends good money after bad.

A word of warning! Do not buy the so-called automatic door latches that come with chain link. They do not always close properly and a moment of carelessness can bring disaster. Buy instead the "U" shaped latches, the kind that lift to open. When you close this latch, you will see a hole underneath in which you can affix a clip. Buy bolt clips from a hardware store — the kind you expect to find on the end of a quality dog lead — and use them every time you close the gate. With the clip in place, the latch cannot be accidentally opened by human or animal. The clips can be a problem for those readers fortunate enough to share cold weather with us. They often freeze shut in the cold weather, especially on days when you are in a hurry. Just warm them with your hands for five or ten seconds and they will eventually open.

"Look," you say, "the man next door chains his dog to a dog-house, or under a tree, and just leaves him there year round." We do not doubt your veracity for a moment. Men beat their wives and children also. If a tree and chain describes what you plan for a dog, do not attempt to purchase from us, or any other reputable breeder. If the best you can do is to chain him outside, now is not the time to own a dog.

"Are there compromises?"

Yes, there are, happily. If you can fence, but cannot afford to do the whole yard, at least fence in an exercise area, five feet by twenty as a minimum.

"Well, my wife is home all day," you say. "Can't we keep Throck in the house and give him lots of exercise on lead?" Sure you can. But remember, that plan involves at least one long trip or two short trips every day, in all kinds of weather. Thousands of apartment dwellers do just what you suggest and the exercise can benefit both handler and animal. Buy good shoes and foul weather gear and go for it.

DOGHOUSE

"Should we provide an outdoor shelter?"

If Throck will only use his fenced yard to answer nature's demands, exercise, and play with the family, you do not really need a doghouse. If he will be out for long periods, especially at times when no human is home to rescue him from sudden weather changes, you must provide a shelter that protects against the extremes of weather that occur in your region. We cannot offer you construction plans for shelters in every part of the country, so try your local agricultural agent, who can often supply plans for shelters suited to the area. We can, however, offer some generalizations to thicken the stew.

No matter where you build, raise the shelter at least three inches off the ground and make sure it is waterproof. In hot climates, on the sides of the house put hinged panels that can be easily opened for additional air circulation. Buy screen and four sheets of ornamental, perforated metal from the hardware store.

Make two sandwiches, using a layer of screen between each two metal sheets, then use those sandwiches to cover the openings that appear when the panels are raised so that when you open them up the house is still defined. Our screen doors are all done using the same method.

For cold climates, use double walls on your house and insulate with fiberglass. The new insulations will not give off fumes, even when wet. Build your house in such a way so that Throck can enter, make a turn around a partition that goes halfway from front to back, and be free of draft in his cedar-filled bedroom.

A bed of cedar shavings, not chips or mulch, provides comfort, keeps dogs and doghouse smelling good, and combats fleas. Shop price on the shavings. We buy three bushel bags and find the price varies widely for the same product. The inside of the house will have to be cleaned periodically, and Throck won't do it. Unless you are a contortionist who enjoys working in confined and cramped spaces, design your house with a removable roof.

A final consideration. Always keep in mind that Throck will chew if he can, especially while a puppy. Unless you enjoy the prospect of building replacement houses, use sturdy materials, and build it to last.

PROTECTING THE YARD

"Are there enticements in the yard?"

You bet! Look at that lovely side porch, for example. Redwood furniture, stuffed cushions, indoor/outdoor carpet! What a feast for a puppy on a chewing spree. The hose becomes a sprinkler, and see that downspout? We also have a well chewed downspout for sale. Our dogs even took it down for us. Your animal will do the same, as well as strip the house of that aluminum or vinyl siding and try his best with clapboards. Concrete block and brick are pretty safe. Protect, or graciously accept the consequences.

"Are there also dangers in the yard?"

Probably, especially if Throck can get into the garage. Petroleum products, such as antifreeze, gas, kerosene, brake fluid, paint thinner, paraffin, insecticide, solvents, and charcoal starter, are all toxic, as are lead-based products such as paint, fishline sinkers, and solder. Store the dog's enemies well out of his reach.

"There's nothing left but the plants and garden!"

Right you are, and with luck, the plants and garden may survive a week — longer if they are under snow. Just because Throck appears to ignore them the first few times out does not mean they are safe forever. He will not understand their importance to you, or their potential danger to him.

First, chase away any toads living in the garden. Several varieties are poisonous. Next, remove any slug or snail bait, then identify all the trees and plants. Many varieties, including the following, can be toxic: apple, apricot, autumn crocus, avocado, azalea, black-eyed susan, black locust, bleeding heart, boxwood, buckeye, buttercup, chinaberry, chokecherry, daphne, English ivy, foxglove, golden chain, hemlock, holly, hyacinth bulbs, jack-in-the-pulpit, lantana, larkspur, lily of the valley, monkshood, mountain laurel, mushrooms, narcissus, nightshade, oak (acorn), oleander, pokeweed, potato, privet, rhododendron, rhubarb, thornapple, tomato, wisteria, yellow jasmine, and yew.

A long list, and quite possibly not inclusive for your area. Check with your poison control center or agricultural agent for other toxic varieties that grow where you live. Either remove the plants and forget the garden, or protect them with a fence.

One last look around. Have you protected everything you consider valuable from Throck? Is Throck protected from everything dangerous to him? Then let's look inside.

INDOOR DANGERS

"Dangers and enticements inside too?"

There are more of both than we could possibly list. Let's start with the dangers. We shall mention a few and let your inventive mind calculate the rest. In the kitchen alone you may well have detergents, water softener, bleach, cleaning solutions, dyes, disinfectants, scouring pads, silver polish, ammonia, drain cleaner, oven cleaner, medicines, cigarettes, and shoe polish. All of the above can be toxic to Throck. Check the other rooms, especially the bath. The whole house is full of enticements for a puppy, such as protruding corners on walls and cabinets, rugs, clothing, shoes, furniture, electric wires, and wallpaper. Give Throck an afternoon to himself and you will not recognize the place.

"You mean all those things are potential targets?"

We do indeed. Take, for instance, our friend who owns an Ibizan that chewed the center out of an heirloom Persian rug, and another friend with a boxer that rearranged his teeth when he bit the electric cord to the freezer. We have lots of memories. Tina, our lovely old Clumber dam, specialized in swiping and devouring deer steaks, cookies, and pumpernickel. She added variety when she helped Danny Boy eat the new calculator. Not that Danny needed help; he chewed the heel off of a guest's shoe while she sat at the table playing a board game and that was just practice for the time he pulled the phone off the wall, dragged it through the doggy door, and chewed it in the mud.

We have many other dogs and could list memories from each, but by now you should understand the point. Human carelessness provides adventures for animals and each adventure provides memories for owners. If Throck can, sooner or later, he will.

THE DECISION

"Do I really want a dog?"

Now is a good time to ask yourself that question. You are considering taking on the responsibility of a living creature, not so different, in many ways, from a child. You may think we purposely painted a black picture, but the truth is, we did not even attempt to tinge it gray. We did not mention illnesses, accidents, disabilities, or deaths. Challenge and responsibility become part and parcel of owning an animal, and increase geometrically as you add more animals.

If you cannot now accept those demands then put this book on the shelf until you can. The problems and heartaches you save yourself, the breeder, and the animal will justify a hundred times over the money you spent for this volume. If you are not ready, just as with the parent who is not ready, the pet can only increase tension, frustration, and guilt.

"Is there a positive side?"

Since you are still reading, we happily announce that many rewards and fulfillments derive from owning a purebred dog. Many! We purposely saved them for last. For most involved with purebreds, animals get third priority, behind immediate family and relatives. For many, they take priority over, or at least equate with, relatives.

Throck will reduce tension in the person who finds himself alone, and comfort that person against depression. He provides someone to talk to, touch, and share positive and negative emotions with. Caring for him and occasionally showing him off will enhance his self-image. Knowing he lies close by will give you a feeling of added security.

If yours is a family setting, a dog will become a welcome addition. He will stimulate more fun, laughter, and conversation, hence reducing family tension. Love for Throck will sharpen the family's capacity for compassion and will promote togetherness.

An animal also offers something to the couple who have not yet experienced children. Taking care of him will teach you the pleasures of both nurturing and physically demonstrated affection.

Perhaps the child, or the child in us, benefits the most. The child learns what it is to have something dependent on him, and in so doing, learns a greater respect for life. It's a two way street. Throck will reward the children and all of the family members, for that matter, with consistent acceptance of them as individuals, regardless of physical and mental capacities, looks, or dress. We cannot presume to speak for you, but we will trade a telephone and some chair rungs for that kind of love any day.

What we have briefly described (and understated), dog literature often refers to as the human/animal bond. The bond must be experienced to be understood and appreciated. Mere words could not do it justice.

So now that you have a larger part of the story, and if you think, as we do, that the potential rewards and fulfillments far outweigh the hazards, let's proceed to the next chapter and get to work finding the right Throck for you.

2.

Breeds and Supplies

Luck favored us when we found and chose our first puppy. Unfortunately for both animals and owners, we know of many whose luck did not treat them so kindly. To put the odds more in your favor, we want to equip you with a systematic approach to use in selecting the right breed for you. It would not hurt, though, to go to a store or library, and secure a book with pictures of all the breeds. We certainly would not deride basing your decision, in part, on aesthetic appeal, for several breeds will undoubtedly catch your eye. Some of those with appeal will be right for you and your circumstances and some will not. A little research may help you avoid buying one of the 'will nots'.

BREEDS OF DOGS

"What is the right breed for me?"

Now, please, do not let us mislead you into thinking we know the idiosyncrasies of every breed. We do not! We can only offer you general observations based on our experience and research. If you fall in love with a breed, verify our information with a breeder.

The American Kennel Club assigns all of the recognized breeds into one of seven groups, each group designating the original purpose for which the breed developed. (Owners of several breeds hotly contest A.K.C.'s assignments.) In the Sporting Group you find hunters and in the Herding Group you find herding dogs. Easy enough, so far. Two more easy ones! Hounds are in the Hound Group; Terriers are classified – as those who dig the 'terra', or earth, in pursuit of rodents – in the Terrier Group. Most large dogs – those intended for pulling carts, or providing protection and rescue – compete in the Working Group. The little guys, bred for apartments and laps, appear in the Toy Group. And then, there are the leftovers; the poodles and bulldogs and such. We delight in taunting friends who own dogs in this category by referring to their animals as the non-dogs. Actually the group is called the Non-Sporting Group.

Knowing the intended function of the breeds offers the first clue to their desirability for you. Hunters require exercise; often, lots of exercise. Shih Tzus and other Toys make poor jogging companions. Many hounds enjoy being outside more than inside. A Terrier will do his best to protect, but will not pose the deterrent that a Rottweiler will. With a little thought, you can draw your own generalizations.

As we move to specifics — drooling, chewing, and the like — remember that this is a list of considerations, not necessarily condemnations. There are no perfect dogs. What bothers some people does not bother others. For example, we accept shedding. If you come to our home, wear scruffy clothing. A trip through the house once a day with the vacuum cleaner solves most of the problem, but we make no promises to those dressed in black velvet.

LOOSE GENERALIZATIONS

Affection. The Sportings, Herdings, Non-Sportings, and Toys tend to be affectionate. Terriers are often a little more feisty and sometimes aggressive. The Hounds tend to be more aloof.

Exercise. Sporting, Herding, and Hound Group dogs all like plenty of daily exercise. Terriers like their share, especially large ones such as the Airedale. Dalmatians and Chows, from the Non-Sports, and Rottweilers, Malamutes, and Boxers, from the Working Group, are ambitious. The Toys, with the possible exception of the English Toy Spaniel and the Italian Greyhound, can exercise themselves in the living room.

Digging. Many of the Sporting, Hound, Working, and Terrier dogs will dig, and not always in the ground. Sports will think nothing of digging a nest in your sofa. With any of the diggers, especially Hounds and Terriers, make sure the bottom of the fence is in a trench.

Chewing. Sports and Hounds provide the worst chewers. Terriers, too, will chew badly when confined for long periods of time. Remember, if they can, they will — especially puppies.

Drool. Many of the Sporting dogs drool moderately. Bloodhounds, Saint Bernards, Newfoundlands, Boxers, and Danes drool a lot!

Shedding. Poodles, Bedlington Terriers, Wheaten Terriers, Boston Terriers, and Portuguese Water Dogs, so we are told, shed little or not at all. Hounds shed moderately. Sport, Herding, some of the Terriers, and the long-haired Working dogs shed profusely. If you fall in love with one of these latter breeds, do not let the shedding worry you. We have three suggestions that will help. Buy a good vacuum cleaner, do not entertain fastidious friends, and purchase lots of clothes that are close in color to your dog.

Training. Almost every dog can be trained. Every dog should be trained, including the Toys. Dobermans, Shepherds, Shelties, Goldens, and Clumbers learn quickly. On the other hand, Danes and Saints are lazy. Chesapeake Bay Retrievers, German Short-haired Pointers, Irish Setters, Weimaraners, Boxers, Yorkshire Terriers, Chihuahuas, Keeshonden, Chow Chows, Lhasa Apsos, Dalmatians, Bulldogs, Borzois, Welsh Springers, most Hounds, and many Terriers qualify as stubborn.

Travel. The difficulty of traveling with animals lessens dramatically when the animals travel in crates. On the loose, Terriers require discipline. Some individual dogs suffer car sickness, especially when young. We experienced just one. A quarter mile from the show site, up came everything she ate over the last six months. Only Carrie and the crate needed cleaning, but with competition an hour away, one crate and one dog to clean is enough. Imagine Carrie and the other animals loose in the vehicle! We could still be cleaning. By the way, the malady lasted about a month. Carrie travels well now.

Barking. We are not talking about the dogs who bark at harsh noises, strangers, or intruders. Most do that. We mean barking. Barking! Barking! Barking! Hounds and Terriers are the worst, or the best, depending how you see it. Toys, especially if confined, rival them, especially in pitch and frequency.

Grooming. Most of the long-haired breeds need brushing regularly, some constantly. The giants, like Danes, can pose problems when it comes to bathing. Several of the Toys and Non-Sports require extensive grooming, as do the Poodles, Chows, Lhasas, Bichons, and Maltese. Schnauzers are tough to groom. Shih Tzus are criminal. We once got duped into watching a tape on the proper grooming of these critters by a friend who breeds them. The woman on the tape spent almost eight hours on just one little skunk size dog. Thankfully they only recorded about two hours worth. Some people love all that work. Give us the good old hour-at-the-most breeds every time. Most any dog can benefit from a daily brushing, if only to let him know you care.

Temperament. Bad breeding so often causes bad temperaments. Shepherds, Rottweilers, Chows, Cockers, and Dobermans, to name a few, have had their ups and downs with temperaments, largely because too many indiscriminate breeders tried to meet the demand for puppies. Irish Setters, Weimaraners, Pointers, Beagles, Afghans, Yorkies, Chihuahuas, Chows, Dandies, Miniature Pinschers, Pekingese, and Kerry Blue Terriers appear to enjoy a good fight with other dogs. Afghans, Basenjis, Foxhounds, Harriers, Greyhounds, Whippets, American Water Spaniels, Borzois, Dandies, Scottish Terriers, Miniature Pinschers, and Pekingese are questionable around children. Chows can be overly protective of children but don't always like other dogs.

Now please, do not take our word as the last for any of the above. If you really want to hear the positives and negatives of a breed, talk to those who own and/or breed them. Will they tell the truth? We would like to think so. We find it difficult to imagine a breeder wanting to place a puppy in the wrong home. Bear with us and we shall tell you how to contact these people, but before leaving this subject on breed choice, another caution. We assume that one day you may also want to breed. Think now to the future. One dog, an hour and more a day for grooming, no problem, but what happens when you have twenty?

And everybody loves puppies. But puppies rapidly become adults. When you choose a breed, look at the adults first, then the puppies. Too many puppies, purebreds included, wind up in the pound because they grew up to be something the owner did not desire, or could not handle.

FINDING BREEDERS

"Where do I find one?"

Let us suppose that you looked at pictures, considered the good points and bad, and decided you must own a Clumber Spaniel. Now you want to talk to a breeder.

You could go to a dog show and hope someone entered Clumbers that day. The catalog will tell you what time they show and in what ring. Wait until after the competition, then talk to the person on the other end of the lead. Hopefully that person will invite you to see other dogs they have at home, or will suggest whom to call to accomplish that purpose. Please remember that many who show dogs do not breed them and may only own the animal you see, or only handle the animal for the owner. Still, they should be able to put you on the right track.

If there is no show coming to your area in the near future, or you go and find no Clumbers, write to the A.K.C. and request the address of the breed club secretary. You will want help from others who own your breed as you progress in the sport. If the secretary or any of the breeders you contact seem unfriendly at the start, perhaps you should reconsider and make another breed selection.

Should the club secretary fail you, buy one of the magazines that devote themselves to dogs. All of them contain advertisements placed by breeders. Contact one of the columnists for specific information on the breed that interests you. An A.K.C. publication entitled *Pure-Bred Dogs/American Kennel Gazette* features breed columns. At the end of each column is the name and address of the columnist. These good people are usually very responsive to inquiries.

Let's assume the following scenario. You contact the club secretary, who in turn puts you in touch with a nearby breeder who has puppies ready for sale, and plenty of adults for you to inspect. (We like to think there are still such things as miracles.) Let us further assume that a purchase is a certainty. Does this mean you are ready to charge off and buy the puppy? No, you are not nearly ready. Not yet. First we need to do a little shopping.

SUPPLIES AND EQUIPMENT

"What supplies and equipment do I need?"

A Crate

First, buy Throck a crate. That bears repeating. Buy Throck a crate! Please, buy Throck a crate! Throck will love you for it, his breeder will love you for it, you will love you for it.

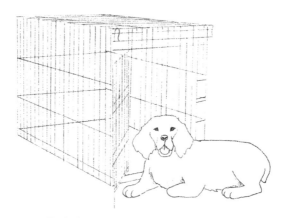

Each dog should have its own crate.

The crate provides Throckmortana with her own room, a place to retreat when she tires of human commotion. Put her in it when Grandma, who hates dogs, comes to visit. Leave her there, within reason, while you work, protecting her and your possessions at the same time. Picture coming home to tattered furniture, shredded wallpaper, and soggy, pulpy cookbooks. If you find the pictures disagreeable, purchase Throck a crate!

Other advantages: the crate is excellent for housebreaking the dog. It also provides a quiet place for her to eat, a bedroom of her own to sleep, and, when she is sick and has to be kept quiet, it becomes a hospital. Wet and muddy? She dries in it; a crate tray washes much more easily than Dad's recliner.

You should have a vehicle that can accommodate an assembled crate to protect the dog against sudden stops, sharp turns, and accidents. And you never know when those accidents will happen. Recently, a friend traveling to a show had her vehicle rear-ended at a light. The crate split, but the concussion only bruised the dog. Also, one day Toni took two Clumbers on a quick trip into town, and let them ride loose in the back of our Trooper. The Trooper never made it back, and even though the dogs survived the wreck unharmed, Toni did not. There she lay in the sleet and snow, holding on to two loose and frightened animals, while the rescue squad ran around trying to figure out what to do with them. She never took dogs anywhere without them in crates again.

At shows the crate provides a haven from spectators and

other animals and a clean place to put the groomed dog ready for the ring. It also affords her a well ventilated confinement while you enjoy the rest of the competition. Too often we see people show their dogs, then stick them back in a hot car for the rest of the day. Even if you do not own a wagon or something bigger, please buy a crate. They disassemble or fold for travel, and you will find motels much more receptive to crated animals in the room.

Please, buy Throck a crate, but never, ever, never, use the crate to punish.

Food

"Food and water?"

You also have to provide Throck with a daily supply of food and water. Let's start with the easier of the two — water. Tap water will do. Some owners who have water softeners think tap water adds too much salt to the dog's diet. If you agree, buy distilled water.

Dogs can have the same problems adjusting to strange water that humans have. When you travel, take a supply of water with you. Two gallon plastic jerry cans, intended for campers, work fine. For short stays, use a gallon milk container, well washed. Forgot his water? No need to panic. Stop at a grocery store or a convenience store and buy distilled water. If you start to run low, add some of the foreign water to his regular brand and gradually build a tolerance. Water is the easy part.

The subject of food takes us into a very complex area in which even the expert nutritionists lack answers. Wet, dry, or semi-dry? Corn base, soy, or meat? How much calcium and phosphorous? Should I supplement? The subject boggles the mind.

Three governmental agencies watch over the dog food industry. The National Research Council prescribes the standards; the Association of Feed Control Officials tests the products on the animals; and the Federal Trade Commission oversees the package labeling. If that makes you feel safe, you are too easily pleased.

The N.R.C. offers standards for an average maintenance diet. This assumes that all dogs, regardless of temperament and environment, require the same balance of nutrients fed to them in greater or lesser amounts. Sounds good, if it is true. We agree that you achieve optimum nutrition when quantity, quality, and balance are in a state of nutritional equilibrium, but we still doubt that anyone can formulate an average maintenance diet. In any event, the Federal Trade Commission insists that the manufacturers label their product in terms of the N.R.C. standards. If the manufacturer complies with the standard, you can be sure they mention that fact on their packages. Easy, this far. Now we get to the glitches.

The food must comply with the standard under chemical analysis. If the label makes claims, it is a good bet that the manufacturer can substantiate those claims with a chemical analysis. Unfortunately, chemical analysis does not assure bioavailability. This simply means that the animal's body can digest and make use of the nutrients offered. If the animal cannot, what happens to balanced nutrition? A testing of generic brands, for example, demonstrated that dogs could only utilize a percentage of the protein level claimed on the label.

Most breeders we know just avoid the morass of misinformation and gamble on one of the nationally prominent brands. The leading companies spend copious amounts of money on research and attempt to deliver an honest product that will still allow them a profit.

Not entirely trusting manufacturers governed by a profit motive, many breeders supplement the standard ration. This could be dangerous! Especially when the breeders react to only the animal's outward appearance and activity, or old wives' tales, or too often, misinterpreted facts. When the balance of vitamins and minerals is disturbed by supplements, what happens to the internal dog?

Protein and fat are the only areas that we sometimes adjust. Protein builds tissue. For an active animal, the average minimum standard may not be enough. An egg is perfect protein, and three eggs a week will offer a protein boost. Raw eggs can be harmful, so to remove all danger, cook the egg. Cottage cheese is also good. If you choose dry food, as we did, be aware that dry foods only include up to 11% or 12% fat. More would bleed through the package. On the days you do not add an egg, you might want to add a teaspoonful of corn oil, which contains linoleic acid. Fat helps transport vitamins A, D, E, and K, as well as supplying energy and of all the fats, linoleic acid is the most important.

Calcium and phosphorus are the minerals needed in the largest quantities. The accepted ratio is 1.2 to 1, calcium to phosphorus. This allows for optimum tooth and bone formation.

A rule of thumb! A five pound dog requires 250 kilocalories per day; ten pounds — 450 kilocalories; thirty pounds — 900; sixty-five — 1600; 150 — 3000. One pound of 11% protein canned food offers roughly 400 kilocalories; 25% protein semi-moist food — 1400 kilocalories; and 24% protein dry food — 1500 kilocalories per pound. If you must err in terms of quantity, err by underfeeding.

On days you supplement with an egg, back off seventy-five kilocalories. The egg more than compensates — your protein content will only increase 1% with the addition of the egg, but your protein value will increase by over 20%.

Our best suggestion is to start with whatever food your breeder uses with success. Add eggs and oil if you feel the need to supplement. Before you dabble with other supplements, check with your vet or the manufacturer as to the possible consequences. It would be helpful if the leading manufacturers supplied hot lines, nutritionists, to answer supplement questions.

"What containers should we use for food and water?"

We tried them all and have a huge graveyard for containers. Anything less than hard plastic usually perishes quickly, and even that looks chewed and grungy after limited use. Marble dishes are lovely, if you have only one dog; try carrying twenty at a time! We settled on stainless steel dishes and pails for food and water. Even puppies do not seem to relish chewing on stainless steel and cleaning is easy.

One other point; we do not believe in food on demand. More about that later. However, we do believe in a constant water supply, and so will Throck.

Toys

"Should I buy toys?"

Throck will believe in a constant supply of toys. When he is a little guy, he will enjoy plastic soft drink bottles and plastic milk jugs with tops and labels removed, but they only work before he is large enough to rip off pieces and devour them. Then use commercial toys. (Manufacturers call them pacifiers.)

For our money, and we've spent lots of it, you cannot beat Cressite™ balls, or the heavy duty nylon rings and bones purchased from pet supply people. The lightweight nylon stuff from the grocery store tends to splinter too easily, and dogs love to play tug-of-war with nylon toys, and chew and chew. Our oldest Clumber boy has a red and white Cressite™ ball he has constantly carried in his mouth for the last four years. You have not lived until you sit quietly reading and hear a dog bounce his Cressite™ ball down wooden steps, then catch and chase the ball as it bounces off the wall at the bottom.

We avoid rawhide bones for larger dogs. They soon unwind the rawhide and devour great hunks, which then lie in the stomach and defy digestion. For the same reason, avoid old sneakers. We saw a Clumber miss death by a hair because a piece of sneaker formed a blockage in his stomach.

If you look for rewards as a dog owner, wait until the first time you come home after a hard day and Throck turns himself inside out trying to find a toy to bring you. Believe us, your day is made.

Collars and Leads

"Will I need a collar and lead?"

You certainly will. Unless in the house or in the confines of a fenced yard, do not ever take your dog out without it. An innocent distraction or a split second of impetuous behavior can put him in that graveyard with the containers and toys. The person who shows off his dog's training by walking him off lead fails to impress us. We are impressed by the person who takes no chances in a world Throck cannot fully understand.

Leads usually come in leather, nylon, or cordo-hyde, a cotton material, and vary in thickness from strings to three-quarters of an inch. We use a variety. As with collars, some dogs seem to prefer one over the other. Most often we use nylon or cordo-hyde in the show ring and leather for obedience work. We have a separate set of nylon and retractable leads that we use for strolling.

In leather, wider is stronger and rawhide is easiest on the hand. Cordo-hyde is exceptionally strong and washable. Nylon comes in a wide variety of colors, and is washable, strong, and cheaper. Six feet makes a flexible length.

Perhaps more important than the quality of the lead is the quality of the clip at the end. Clips come in three basic types. The German, or bolt clip, will break under stress, but is less likely to do so than the others. The French, or seeing-eye clip, opens bilaterally. They are good when they are new, but age and stress weaken them. Spring clips are common, but they too will weaken with age and give out under stress, even when new. Which clip you should purchase will in large part depend on the size and strength of Throckmortana. To be on the safe side, we use only German clips.

No question about it, chain choke collars provide a faster response time. When you jerk on the lead, the collar tightens faster around Throck's neck if it is chain. The flat links work faster than the rounded and have less tendency to hang up on themselves. They also cut the coat around the neck better than do the rounded. If you select chain, remember that many of them rust. Look out for a blue cast, which indicates nickel and will not last. And spending more for chrome does not get you out of the woods completely. Though it is as good as chains get, it can discolor the coat.

The best nylon collars are woven and sewn. Again, they come in multiple colors, are strong, and are washable. On the negative side, they gray with use and provide a slower response time.

Not everyone uses lead-collar combinations. We often use a martingale, a lead and collar all in one. They serve well for training puppies of any breed. If the dog is an adult, the martingale will still assist him in maintaining balance. We have only seen them in nylon. In fitting a martingale, make sure the rings are still two inches apart when you snug the collar.

We might also mention that some handlers favor the French humane choke collar. It is made to stop closing short of choking the animal, no matter how much pressure is exerted. And many handlers use what is called a slip lead for the Toy breeds. They work well for the smaller dogs, especially if equipped with a swivel that prevents the lead from twisting.

Usually the color of the lead and collar blends with the color of the dog, but not always. If you have a breed that emphasizes the head of the dog, a contrasting color will make the head look larger. Avoid the tried and true strap and buckle collar that remains on the dog all the time. It is not for show dogs. The collar wears a permanent ring around the dog's neck that will not be received well in the show ring. We never leave collars of any kind on our dogs. Especially, never leave on a choke. Throck can snag a choke on something and throttle herself before you can come to the rescue.

Our observations: Terrier, Sporting, and Non-Sporting breeds usually show on chain chokes, nylon chokes, martingales, or slip leads. Hounds are on nylon or chain chokes with nylon leads, sometimes leather. Working and Herding dogs appear most often on chain chokes with leather, nylon, or cordo-hyde leads. Toy handlers seem to prefer martingales or slip leads.

In the final analysis, the combination that allows you and Throck to work as a team wins. Do not overdo her restraint; too much restraint raises questions. Once we saw Rottweiler handlers arrive at a show with animals that wore two-inch-wide collars on the end of something that approached anchor chain. They sure made us wonder about the quality of temperament they bred.

Have we forgotten anything? We tried not to. But we do seem to be missing something! Of course — Throck! We got so excited with all that preparing, we almost forgot the star. Well, we can remedy that. Let's go buy your puppy.

3.

Puppy Shopping

Let's review a moment to make sure authors and readers are still moving in the same direction and at the same speed. After much fact- and soul-searching to select the breed best suited to your family, you exercised incredible wisdom and chose the Clumber Spaniel. (That you, at the same time, made it easier for the authors by choosing the Clumber, is pure coincidence.)

You decided against trying to track down a breeder at a show. As we mentioned, unless you want one of the popular breeds, you might not find your breed there. Instead you wrote to the American Kennel Club requesting the name of the secretary of the Clumber Spaniel Club. Those of you who chose another breed asked for the appropriate secretary's address.

Once you received the secretary's name and address, you wrote to her expressing your interest in the breed and requesting names of breeders who may have puppies for sale. To your surprise, you received only one name and that was of breeders five or six hours away. Whether you realize it or not, you did very well.

For the sake of clarity, let us take all the breeds recognized by A.K.C. and assign them to one of three groups — popular breeds, semi-popular breeds, rare breeds. The numbers of puppies registered with A.K.C. each month are in the thousands for the popular breeds. The semi-popular breeds will register puppies numbering in the hundreds each month, and the rare breeds, with luck, only in the tens. To elaborate, in the month of December 1989, A.K.C. registered 7,615 Cocker Spaniels, 102 English Cocker Spaniels, and 3 Clumber Spaniels. To offer another example, 3,595 Cocker litters, 39 English Cocker litters, and 3 Clumber litters were registered in the same month.

We hope the numbers make our point. If your choice of breed falls in the popular group, your chances of locating a nearby breeder, with available puppies, are a thousand times better than our poor mythical reader in search of a Clumber.

That is not to say there are puppies always available upon demand, even in the popular breeds. We always chuckle over those who call and want a pet Clumber for their brother's birthday the following week. No quality breeder in his right mind would breed often enough to have a constant supply of puppies available. None that we know of anyway.

Many breeders establish waiting lists. The rarer the breed, the longer the list. To purchase a pet puppy out of one of the rare breeds may require a wait of two years or more.

How the purchase continues from this juncture will obviously vary widely depending on breed and breeder of choice, availability, and proximity. Again we cannot pretend to cover all the possibilities.

If your breeder is across country, for example, you must obviously deal with extra problems – shipping, reliance on the breeder's choice, etc. These problems are easily worked out with an experienced breeder and can also be worked out with a novice. Whether by phone, mail, personal visit, or other means, the breeder must receive enough information to trust you with the animal. You must receive enough information to purchase, raise, and enjoy your new family member.

The best we can do is offer you a model of what we expect during a puppy purchase, with an emphasis on the information exchanged. To make that easier, let's pretend our Clumber enthusiast wrote to us and we had one bitch show puppy still available from our most recent litter. What follows, then, is what we expect to happen. We did make one modification. To clarify the flow of events for the reader, we combined those events to all take place during one customer visit. Actually, we prefer Clumber customers to make at least two visits for pets and we ask show quality purchasers also to meet us at one show. Like all models, the actual meeting usually differs.

CHOOSING THE BREEDER

"What should I know about the breeder?"

As much as you can. When you make that appointment with the breeder for a time when neither of you will be rushed, ask for some information. First, ask whether the Clumber is their only breed and note any additional breeds. Ask for the names of three or four of their previous customers. If there are none to offer, you now have an assessment of their experience. Inexperience is not necessarily negative; only worry if the breeder sounds irritated and reluctant to furnish names. Good breeders want you to hear their praises sung by former clients.

While you wait for the appointment day do some homework. First contact the A.K.C. and inquire if anyone ever filed a complaint against the breeder. Next, if they breed multiple breeds, contact the secretaries of those breed clubs to ask whether the breeder maintains good standing. Finally, call those former customers. Believe us, only the unusual dog person will conceal negatives relating to a breeder. Happily, even though the breeder may be a primary competitor, most will also be up front with positives.

If you receive any information that sounds negative, confront the breeders and listen to their side. Still not satisfied? Write the breed secretary and request another name. Farther away does not matter if it makes you more comfortable.

"What will the breeder want to know about me?"

Nervous already? There is no need to be. The breeder wants you to be a wonderful prospect who can provide a fitting home for a very dependent animal. The breeders love their puppies. If they make a mistake, they prefer to err on the side of caution.

When you arrive at our home and before you are introduced to any of the animals, "up-close and personal," as they say, we will invite you to relax in the living room and chat. We might break the ice by asking you whether you previously owned a dog, which is a simple question, easily answered. We always prefer to see the head shake from side to side. There is more to teach the novice owner, but no bad habits or misinformation to correct. If the person describes a previous experience negatively, he alerts us. Compound that negative experience with information that the animal died through neglect, and conversation ends as soon as courtesy allows, or more abruptly. Do not call us, we'll call you.

Are there children in the family? Are they excited about a puppy? We worry when the head bobs up and down, but the potential owner comes alone. We like to see the whole family involved with a puppy, pet or show quality. Yet many times, especially with show dogs, we see only one family member participate. That works, as long as the other family members do not turn hostile to the idea. Human antagonism, especially from a jealous child, can spell misery for a helpless puppy.

When we agreed to let you come and see a dog, we calculated that you had three things going for you. First, you expressed an interest in Clumbers and second, you lived reasonably close. (We love to place puppies in close enough proximity that we get to see them now and again.) The third attribute, especially important when discussing a show quality animal, was your enthusiasm, your desire to show the animal. It also raises a question that many breeders get too embarrassed to ask. Can you afford it? Considering the cost of puppyproofing, puppy purchase, and vet bills, added to travel and show expenses, the question seems appropriate.

At this point in the conversation, if we all still agree the conversation should be continued, we open five or six crates containing adult Clumbers who want nothing more than to love new friends. We do not expect the buyers to wrestle on the floor with them, though many wind up there. Neither do we want to see the prospective buyers back into a corner and spend the remainder of their stay picking hair from their clothing.

Why do we use this tactic? For a couple of reasons. Everybody loves a puppy; but puppies grow into adults, and we want to know how new owners will relate to the full size dog. And while they are preoccupied and probably off guard, we like to slide in our last question, concerning future plans. If we sell a show quality bitch, we want her shown. Handle her yourself, meet us at a show so we can handle her for you, or have a professional show her. We shall also contract that she be bred at least once. Especially in a rare breed, the genes of show quality bitches cannot be wasted. Just think, when that day comes, and you have a litter to watch over, you will ask these questions of someone.

"How can we assess the breeder?"

The breeder who plays down the importance of the health and quality of the puppy's parents, should leave you ill at ease. If the discussion of the puppy's quality rests only on the fact that the parents are registered with A.K.C., get nervous. That can mean merely that someone registered the parents with that organization. Contrary to what those little advertisements in the newspaper and many pet store owners would have us believe, registration with A.K.C. says absolutely nothing about the health and quality of the animal, nor does it deny the possibility of bad temperament and multiple defects. Again, A.K.C. registration simply means the alleged parents of the puppy are purebreds and known to the A.K.C.

Worse is the breeder who avoids any discussion of the parents, cannot present them, or cannot produce reasonable photographs. Quite possibly your alleged breeder is more alleged than actual breeder. If the sellers can produce nothing about the puppy's parents beyond names, the animal for sale probably came from a puppy mill, a place where the objective is mass production, and little or no attempt is made to screen and eliminate genetic defects. The puppies, after receiving minimal human contact, are shipped to the sales point at a very early age, often under traumatic conditions. The plump little dog that catches your eye in the window may in truth be bloated with parasites. The puppies usually sell at bargain prices, or what appears to be a bargain. The handicap of proceeding without background information, the value of heartaches, and the cost of vet bills, added to the sum of the purchase price make the bargain disappear.

THE PUPPY'S BACKGROUND_____

"How important is heritage?"

We think, for the show puppy purchaser, that it is extremely important. The pet puppy buyer gets a short course, because that animal will be spayed or neutered. The show animal owner, however, needs to know how to evaluate his animal against its competition. And the show animal will eventually be bred, so for that person, heritage is very important, whether the buyer realizes it at this stage or not.

After chatting and answering questions, the buyer wants to see the puppy. Not yet. First, we prefer to introduce the buyer to the puppy's relatives. That requires a walk — the yard, downstairs, upstairs, wherever they happen to be.

Once we locate the puppy's relatives, we supply the customer with a five generation pedigree to guide them through time. Next they receive an introduction to the relatives in residence: parents, grandparents, great-grandparents, etc. In cases where we do not own some of the animals in the line, or a relative left us for milkbone heaven, we try to furnish photographs.

If every name on the pedigree carries a Ch. prefix (Ch. signifying Champion) you may genuinely feel impressed. Not awed, but impressed. Champions have produced many mediocre offspring. Non-champions have produced many Champions. The fact that few, several, or all of the names in the pedigree lay claim to Championship credentials may, or may not, be important.

Gaining some sense of what appears to pass consistently from generation to generation is important. Hopefully, dominant genes, responsible for recognizable characteristics, have consistently passed through at least three generations, mother's or father's side, to the puppy Throckmortana. Even more important is the hope that those characteristics compare favorably with the standard.

THE STANDARD

"The standard? What standard?"

The club representing each breed composes a pictorial and verbal description of the animal, which could be considered to be the ideal representative of that breed. Theoretically, through careful breeding, the ideal is attainable. Once the description is accepted by the A.K.C., it becomes the official standard. Breeders breed to attain it. Judges use it as a measure.

Until the last few years, when someone asked about the standard we used to whip out the book of A.K.C. standards and flip the pages to show that a written standard existed for nearly every dog. Now, not to be thought out of step with high technology, we produce the tape prepared by the A.K.C. as a pictorial/verbal explanation of the breed standard and plunk it in the VCR.

A standard is available, in writing, on film, or both. Written by whom? By a committee of breed club members. Often, but not always (allowing for politics), the committee members represent the most experienced, knowledgeable, and breed-concerned members in the club.

At the same time, these committee members may well be rivals within the breed, friendly or otherwise, each with his own interpretation of the standard. Not surprisingly, the animals sitting in the respective kennels of those committee members all illustrate the standard, as the kennel owner interprets it. The animals might in fact be quite dissimilar.

Little wonder that differences in interpretation exist. To clip a phrase from a standard, by way of example: "the animal should be long and low." What does one do with such a phrase? Let ten, a hundred, a thousand different people breed and select based on that rather obscure language and you can imagine the result.

Unfortunately the language of the standard does not always improve after subsequent committees meet to revise. Reluctant to change words and create a standard with which the animals they love at home could not comply, new members, on new committees, vote either to keep the existing language or compromise it into even more obscure generalizations.

We try to point out to the prospective buyer the areas in which the puppy's ancestors comply with our interpretation of the standard, and what departures we tried to remedy. If anyone ever bred a perfect dog, we missed it. We shall have more to say about standards and their usage later. On to puppies!

SELECTING THE PUPPY

"How do I select a puppy?"

Often times *you* do not select a show puppy. The *breeder* selects, relying on experience and instinct, formal testing even, to place a puppy in the environment best suited to it. Especially in those cases where the breeder is across country, you have little choice but to rely on the breeder's judgment.

The situation does not improve much for the Clumber buyer in our model. (We need to give her a name. Something exotic. Lynnedora. Lynnedora showing Throckmortana. It has a ring to it.) Evaluate the puppy chosen, then accept or reject it.

"I don't know how to do that," Lynnedora complains.

We do not always know either. Some breeders contend they can select the pick of the litter while the puppies are still wet. They make far better puppy judges than we. They have the fantastic good fortune to breed puppies that always hold together into adulthood, blossoming apace into sensational adults.

When we judge a litter, we first eliminate any puppies with

obvious faults in terms of the standard. We then watch the others play with littermates, checking attitude, movement, adherence to type. Then comes the final test. We walk into the area and the puppy still under consideration that comes out of the pack and unties shoelaces may well stay. This is not very precise help for Lynnedora as she confronts Throckmortana. She has our word that the puppy conforms to type and is structurally sound.

Those are the qualities of the average show dog, the caliber of animal that wins some and loses some. Having seen the parents and such, she can judge whether she thinks the animal appears to possess the traits that appealed to her in the adults.

If she wants a show dog that is better than average, that wins a lot and loses a few, Lynnedora needs to look for signs that the animal has heart. It appears to us that the difference between the marginal and above average show dog lies in the animal's willingness to go all out for his handler in the ring.

Then, too, there is the superior show dog. Every breeder longs for one. Few ever produce one. Take the best of the above average dogs and add that arrogance possessed by all super athletes, the quality that refuses to accept defeat. The result is the superior show dog. Barring politics and bad luck, you will see him standing next to the Best in Show trophy at Westminster.

Lynnedora gets on her hands and knees and stares at the puppy. At that moment little Throckmortana bounds across the room and leaps into her lap. Tongue laps and tail rotates and her eyes ask Lynnedora to take her home. Lynnedora cuddles the baby into her arms and the selection process ends. The woman smiles again, certain she just selected the Best in Show bitch to complete her Westminster fantasy. Stranger things have happened.

Lynnedora's method is probably the most common. But, there are other methods, and we want to discuss two of them. The Puppy Aptitude Test is perhaps the extreme opposite of Lynnedora's emotional approach. Our method falls somewhere in between.

The Puppy Aptitude Test

It is not our intention to describe the entire format for the Puppy Aptitude Test. The information is easily obtained. More than once the *Gazette* has featured it, including the March 1985 issue. We feel confident the A.K.C. Library could furnish you with a copy.

There is even a movie called *Puppy Aptitude Testing.*

Essentially the test works as follows. On day forty-nine of the puppy's life, a day determined by EEG testing, which concludes that all puppies have the brain waves of adults on this day, but are minimally affected by experience and learning thus far, testing begins. Even a day later, according to the originators of the test, environmental experiences may invalidate a "true reading of behavioral tendencies."

An evaluator, a stranger to the puppies, subjects them to a ten part examination, in an unfamiliar location, over a fifteen minute time span. Supposedly, all variables — fatigue, weather, strange scent, etc. — are calculated and accounted for in the result.

The tests are not difficult. In one, the evaluator stands up and walks away from the pup. If it bounds after her and bites at her feet, it is a one. If the pup goes the other way, it is a six. In fifteen minutes, ten tests can measure the degree of social attraction, following dominant or submissive tendency, acceptance of social dominance, acceptance of dominance while in position of no control, willingness to work with a person, sensitivity to touch, sensitivity to sound, intelligent response to strange objects, and structural soundness. Now if that is not a day's work well done, we do not know what is!

When the scores are tabulated, the breeder knows exactly how to place the puppies. Those of us involved in conformation — those competitions which judge the animals against the breed standard — really need only to apply the results of the first five tests. As we understand the scoring, a puppy that scores mostly ones is dominant/aggressive and should only be placed with an exceptionally competent handler, which is in itself difficult to define. Twos are dominant/self-confidents that can be provoked to bite. With experienced and consistent handling they will adapt to a household. Threes, the active/bouncies make wonderful show and house dogs for all but the timid novice. Fours are old Spots, they won't make superior show dogs, but they'll excel as pet and friend. Fives belong with elderly couples who make few demands. Sixes are aloof to people and will seldom be overtly affectionate or responsive.

Although it may seem strange, we recommend purchasing fours. While a three may seem more desirable, for a novice that is a mistake. Threes are still a challenge and too often wind up being a leader of the pack. As we will see in Chapter Four, the human needs to become the leader of the pack in order to properly train a show dog. Fours will win some and lose more but they are much more easier to start with, and if the owner tires of the competition, a four becomes a comfortable pet.

In fairness, we have to say that we hope the test never fails and that one day all puppies will be so accurately tested. But we have to wonder about some of the premises, consistency of evaluators, validity, and reliability of results. It does seem difficult to classify all puppies so easily.

A Compromise Method

For Lynnedora, because Throck is well past forty-nine days of age, she will still have to accept the breeder's word that the test was administered correctly by person or persons competent to interpret the result. This brings us to our method. Whether a litter or single puppy, we look for those who do not appear disinterested or afraid. In no hurry, we carefully examine those that interest us for any signs of ill health. Discharges from nose, eyes, or ears could signal infection, conjunctivitis, or entropian, and distemper. Teeth should be examined for bite configuration, or the proper alignment of the teeth per the standard. Some standards call for scissor bites — uppers over lowers. Some want level bites, others reverse scissors, or lowers in front of uppers. While checking bite configuration, we look for shiny-clean teeth in pink gums. Pale teeth or white gums indicate parasites. A listless puppy with a fat belly — parasites or distemper. Coats should be glossy and fluffy, if long haired.

If a puppy sits there and continually jerks and shakes his head, or paws at his ears, we suspect ear mites. We like to lift pups and stroke their throats. If a chest rumbles or cough follows, the baby may have roundworms, kennel cough, or distemper. As a final precaution, we search for signs of diarrhea, an indicator that the animals may have parasites or coccidiosis. Please do not take a sick puppy home. With good fortune and a good vet, you may help it, but you endanger your other animals. And what of the puppies left behind? Who helps them? Better that you should confront the breeder with your findings and insist he remedy the situation at once. If you encounter opposition, report him to the local dog authorities, the A.K.C., the breed club, and the local kennel club.

Assuming the good health of the animals, the next step is to untie shoe laces and try to lead them to somewhere other than the safe environment of their litter mates. If curiosity prevails, we play ball and exchange kisses. Once the puppy appears comfortable, we lift him and cradle him in our arms, stomach up. If he still gives kisses, he is probably what we want.

One more run to check for straight fronts and driving rears and a brief stack to assess angulation. If the animal's elbows turn out, or the feet point in a direction other than forward, the front is not straight. The rear legs of many animals do little more than hold up their rears. When a dogs has drive, the rear legs thrust the dog forward. Angulation refers to the angle at which the bones meet the knee joint. Usually the standards describe the ideal angulation for the breed.

Many times deficiencies in fronts, rears, and angulation are subtle and apparent only to the experienced eye. The place to start your experience is with your first puppy. If at all possible, take a veteran dog person with you and learn as you purchase. You will also be surprised to find how honest breeders are about their show dogs. They do not want you to be unhappy with your purchase.

"Does it really make any difference whether I buy a male or a female puppy?"

An often asked question. Our answer is yes and no, depending on what you aspire to and what you can tolerate. Males, as a rule, grow larger, are prone to marking their territory with urine, do not get along well with other males when there are bitches about, and win in the show ring more often than females. A bitch presents a heat cycle to contend with twice a year, but she can also provide you with a litter. If you plan eventually to have multiple animals, perhaps even a full scale breeding program, emphasize bitches and keep the males to a minimum.

"Should I consider an adult dog?"

Another popular question, and also a more complex question than it appears. Most often, if an adult dog is offered, it is a finished champion or a pet. Less often, circumstances such as divorce, economic reversal, or exceeded kennel capacity sometimes force competitive animals onto the market. Judge the adult with the same criteria you would use for a puppy. It may take a little longer to bond with the adult animal than with a puppy, but that will come with patience.

Watch out, however, for the adult that is still competitive and appears on the market for no apparent good reason. It may be that the animal has personality problems and cannot get along with its owner, or its kennel mates. Some dogs refuse to accept the canine label and think of themselves as people. Before you consider such an offering, review your future plans. If they include multiple animals, the newcomer may well cause you and your animals problems also.

THE PAPERWORK

"She is in my lap. Is she mine yet?"

She is only a half pound of paper and a half pound of advice away. It won't take long. The first document is a written sales agreement, two pages long. The terms of a sales contract vary with almost every breeder who uses one. Essentially they all describe the animal, state the terms of the sale, and outline the areas of health for which the breeder takes responsibility.

Future considerations are also detailed. Several sections deal with breeding. Down the road, after Throck becomes a champion, these paragraphs pertaining to choice of stud and division of litter will become important. When that time comes and the passage of time has dimmed memories, the involved parties can turn to their written contract for reference.

Every breeder, should supply a health record. Whether vaccinations were given by breeder or vet, the new owner will need this history. The puppy's age, when you take her, will largely decide what information the card contains. We keep our pups for sixteen weeks, thus we vaccinate four times. At five weeks they get the first shot DA2MP, protecting against distemper, hepatitis, adenovirus type 2, and parainfluenza. At seven, nine, and eleven weeks they receive DA2PL-CPV, which also protects against leptospirosis, L. icterohaemorrhagiae, and parvovirus. At that time, we urge the new owner to take the puppy to their vet for a thorough exam and rabies immunization. If vaccinations are not complete, we strongly recommend that you ask for a written two week guarantee against distemper.

The five generation pedigree document we have already described and utilized. Should your breeder fail to supply this important information, you may secure it in part from the A.K.C. They provide a three generation pedigree for fifteen dollars (twenty dollars with the colors of the ancestors), and four generations at twenty-five dollars (thirty-two with colors).

One more piece of paper; for this puppy, white with purple border – your A.K.C. registration certificate. Until January 1, 1990, all buyers of pet puppies and show puppies received one of these. Now pet owners receive a white certification with an orange border, signifying that offspring of that animal are not eligible for registration.

"That seems harsh. Why can't puppies be registered?"

When a breeder designates an animal as a pet, in their judgment, that animal should not be reproduced. It may be that the pet shows minor faults such as wrong color, crooked teeth, or long muzzle. A pet could also display major problems, questionable temperament being among them. Major or minor faults, the breeder believes these traits might well be passed along, disqualifying more and more puppies from the show ring and reversing positive directions in the breed. Unfortunately, in the past, many breeders sold puppies with A.K.C. registration slips and trusted the buyers to support the breeder's wishes by refraining from breeding. We never did. Perhaps we lacked faith in our buyers, but we never released papers until the pet owner supplied us with a vet's certificate of neutering or spaying. As you can imagine, those actions make subsequent breedings difficult.

Too often the owners of pets bought from those more trusting breeders later decided, whether for money, prestige, experience, or something else, that they wanted to breed. As a result, lots of puppies, many with serious faults, cycled into the show rings carrying their bad recessive genes. When overeager novices bred their animals with them, more faulted animals appeared. In short order, whole breeds were undermined.

Pressure finally moved A.K.C., breeders can now sell a pet with a restricted registration. The orange and white certificate clearly states that puppies of that animal will not be recognized. That still will not do the job as thoroughly as requiring spaying or neutering, but it should preclude those who would breed for money or vanity only.

ADVICE

"I can't expect you or any other breeder to be available every minute of every day to answer my questions or help with my problems. Are there others I can go to for help?"

Hopefully! You will need someone to tell you little things as problems arise. Alfalfa tablets stop animals from eating feces. Undergarment guards often work well as doggy bloomers during Throck's seasons. Such tidbits from experienced dog people can make owning and raising a show dog a whole lot easier.

With only slight reluctance, we suggest you contact the kennel club operating in your area. Now the "hopefully" comes in. Hopefully you will contact a dedicated group, such as the Altoona Area Kennel Association in Pennsylvania. We can speak with confidence about that group, because that is our club. They are knowledgeable, caring, and sharing members who do well by the animals and the people who own them.

Remember that we promised only a model for purchase, a description of the way we would like to see it happen every time. It does not always happen that way. Before you contact the breeder, review this chapter. The priorities in the sequence should become obvious. Stand your ground on the essentials, and flex over the secondaries. The bottom line — a love connection between puppy and new family.

We know we spent a lot of time in this chapter, and we did so purposely. The choice you make at the breeders may well determine your future in the sport. We wish we could help you even more.

4.

Puppy Training

"Home with the puppy — at last. Why do I get the feeling that the next step is more complicated than just enjoying her?"

Because, Lynnedora, the next step is more complicated. We certainly champion the family enjoying Throck as much and as often as they can. But some well thought out and carefully planned education for the animal — quickly learned and well received — will allow you to enjoy her even more. We can take that a step further and promise that the education will also enable Throck to enjoy you and the family more. She wants to please the new pack leader and be accepted by the pack. If she understands what is expected, she will work hard to win acceptance.

The education of the animals who remain with us is divided into four phases. In human terms we might refer to elementary school, junior high, high school, and college. More apropos to dogs, let's refer to the four phases of a dog's education as den training, social training, conformation training, and campaign training. (Please remember that this volume and the next emphasize purebreds and conformation training. Those who wish to pursue competitive obedience might also consider tracking and field competition.)

BASIC TRAINING METHODS

"Where do we start?"

Lynnedora will have an advantage over many new owners because we raise puppies in our kitchen. The practice makes each trip across the kitchen a test of courage and pain tolerance for humans. Puppies love to bite toes and ankles to get attention. And we suffer extensive damage to walls, floors, and furniture as a result. Still, the benefits of the constant exposure to the humans and older animals who pass through that room each day more than offset the negatives. When the puppies leave us, they are partially socialized and easily absorbed into a new pack.

Many breeders, however, deprive their puppies of that socialization — the repeated contact with humans and other animals, the daily parade through the kitchen. Instead they raise their litters in basements, garages, and barns. The only adult dog the pups see is their mother. Sometimes days pass without more than hurried human contact. These puppies can present extra problems until they learn to trust.

Whatever the background, start from the premise that all puppies are pack animals by instinct. From the minute it leaves the litter, the puppy searches out a new pack, a pack that it can join or lead. Note the two possibilities. Join or lead!

From the very first moment the puppy enters the new den, a human must assert himself as leader of the pack. The pack leader's authority must prevail, whether the puppy likes it or not. One human or twenty, if not one takes command, the puppy will. Problems then will increase dramatically. That is not to say that the human should take advantage of size and strength to become a tyrant. The puppy is intended to be a friend and a welcome member of the pack. For a successful result as much responsibility falls to the teacher as to the student.

As with children, once Throck learns basic manners, she becomes a social animal. Spoiled puppies, in addition to being obnoxious, often become biters. Unfortunately, many animal owners, too busy or uncaring to train, solve the problem of a puppy's bad manners by putting the animal outside and ignoring it. The neglected animals inevitably become shy and aloof. Many become autistic. We should not be surprised by this behavior in reaction to the owner's treatment. Observe the connection between many ill-mannered children and the way their parents treat them.

Before you attempt lesson one, evaluate your puppy once again. Remember the puppy testing, the ones, twos, threes, and others in the puppy aptitude testing? What those numbers really pertain to are the levels of aggressive and submissive behavior discernible in the animals.

An aggressive dog must never win. You may discipline or ignore the behavior. Never, ever praise it. By way of contrast, the submissive dog tries to make itself smaller, crouching with its tail down, ears back and flat. Expose this animal to other people and animals as soon as possible. Be gentle, make it fun. Praise often and never punish.

"I have a problem already," laments Lynnedora. "Neither of those descriptions fits Throck."

Refer to that circumstance as a blessing, not a problem. The closer Throck comes to the middle distance between those two descriptions, the easier her training will be.

The ground rules apply to the advanced training as well as the elementary. Take every opportunity to reinforce your leadership role by insisting she get your permission before eating, going out, training, or playing. As you train, be consistent. Practice your part first before you invite her out. Be patient. Her progress will depend on your ability to communicate what is expected. Once she understands, repetition strengthens her. That does not imply obsession.

Offer variety in the routine. Sameness, session after session, will dull her enthusiasm, as will lengthy outings. We find that several short sessions are better than one long one. Our animals always seem to train better before meals than after them. Again, do not get carried away. Four sessions of five minutes each should be the outside limit.

Never take your animal out if you feel tired and irritable. Never, ever, never inflict pain. Clothing should not interfere. It is difficult for the dog to concentrate if shoes are squeaking or skirts are slapping her in the face. Smoking is dangerous, for you and your dog.

Above all, be kind. Tomorrow she may have forgotten what she appeared to understand today. You probably did too when you were in elementary school. How many times did you forget to take out the garbage or clean your room?

"Are there several approaches to training?"

There are several, yes, but they are all variations of two. There are different opinions as to which approach is superior. Suffice to say that one school, the one we currently attend, prefers the praise approach. Avoid threats! The word "no" is the only allowable reprimand. Spend some time on the ground, at the dog level, and see the world as she does. Praise emphatically! Demand only what she understands.

The other group advocates disciplining errors quickly, usually by jerking a choke collar closed. They point out that discipline, the mildest correction that works, does not equate with punishment. Give timely corrections, then forgive and hug. Build confidence and love.

Whichever method you prefer, employ it consistently. Remain alert for responses such as nose stabs or hip and body bumps. Such actions are seldom accidents. Do not pass up the opportunity to communicate.

DEN TRAINING

Although we shall discuss all parts of this phase singularly, we do not intend the readers to think the parts should be accomplished one after the other in the sequence presented. That approach will work as a format in the other phases, i.e., social training, show training, and campaign training. It will not work here! Not during den training. Remember, this is elementary school. More probably you will find yourself addressing all the parts, every day, often simultaneously.

Please, whatever else may transpire, never forget for an instant that the puppy's priority in life is pleasing the pack leader. If you communicate properly and consistently, the puppy will respond properly and almost consistently.

Lead Training

If you are lucky, the breeder will have lead trained the puppy before releasing it. Probably you will be unlucky. We know that you and most puppy owners want to get quickly into housebreaking, but that is next to impossible with an animal who is not first accustomed to the lead.

Do not burden the puppy with one of those heavy leather leads that overpower the baby. Use a nylon choke collar and nylon lead, just heavy enough to give you command and to restrain the animal.

As soon as you get her home, attach the lead and allow her to drag it around the kitchen. After a few minutes, lift her. Be sure to carry a puppy properly. If she is of any size at all, support her hindquarters. With a large puppy, use your arms like the blades of a forklift. Put one arm in front of her forelegs and one behind the rear legs. The idea here is to support both ends and the middle.

Carry the pup, still wearing the lead and collar, to some spot a short distance from the house. Set her on the ground. Give her a minute to explore or cower, then coax her toward the house. Persuade her with a cookie, baby talk, gentle tugs with the leash — whatever it takes. Sometimes puppies pick up the idea right away. Sometimes they don't. Be patient and praise good effort.

Let puppy get used to a lead by dragging it around.

Even after she appears to have the idea, prepare yourself for an occasional balk. And, too, she well may expect you to believe she forgot everything she learned the previous day. When it smooths out and the mind games are over, take her for walks often, as reinforcement. Get her used to moving with your left foot, starting when it starts and stopping when your left foot joins the right and stops.

Housebreaking

Usually people use this term to mean the training of the puppy to eliminate its wastes outside. The term does include that training, but in its broader context it also includes the puppy's overall adjustment to his new quarters and new routine.

If you did not hear our plea and did not purchase a crate, gaining the upper hand and housebreaking will be that much more difficult. We will assume you return home with your puppy just before time for the family to retire.

Whether you intend to crate her or not, start establishing your dominance by taking Throck to the area outside where you prefer she eliminate. Walk her on lead until she does eliminate and then praise her. Return with her to the kitchen and allow her to play for another ten or fifteen minutes. If an accident occurs, say no, and return with her to the outside area.

Double check her den for anything destructible, harmful, or both. If you bought one of those cute beds, it probably will not last long. Some animals are allergic to carpet remnants. For the first few days, we shorten the length of the crate by dropping in a partition. Allow just enough room for the animal to lie comfortably. By doing so, the puppy will not get the idea that she can defecate in the rear of the den, while still having a clean front of the crate for eating and sleeping.

Confine her wherever it is you plan to confine her. Let her out, put her back, give her something to eat, let her out and back in again. You reinforce two things at the same time here. You show Throck she must do what you want. At the same time she learns that her den, within the larger den, offers no threats. Let her run in and out of the den several times, then show her the way to the door. Do not hurry her. Let her sniff well.

If you suspect she was not brought up in a crate, feed her with the crate door open. She will soon learn that the new den is hers and does not threaten her. At the end of three or four days – a week at the most – you should be able to remove the partition and close the door while she eats. The crate-raised dog will convert to this immediately.

"What happens if she cries the first night?"

Those of you who are confining your animal to some designated area other than a crate may well toss and turn and wish for earplugs. If you have a towel with the scent of her litter mates on it, wrap it around a tick-tock clock and put it in her bed. With luck, she will accept the ticking as the heartbeats of her pack and settle down. Do not – even if neighbors and police pound on the door – take her into your bed with you. To do so tells her that creating a disturbance gains her what she wants. At the same time, you place your leadership role in jeopardy.

Moving the crate is allowed. If Throck gets lonely the first two or three nights, move the crate into the bedroom at night. You still dominate because she remains confined to her den. Still, she has the security of knowing that pack mates sleep nearby.

9/492

AULT PUBLIC LIBRARY
AULT, COLORADO

One person must take primary responsibility for the training. To our way of thinking, that should be the person who will handle her in the show ring. In this case, Lynnedora. Now that does not mean she would do all the work herself. But it does mean she must coordinate the adventure. Helpers should be assigned tasks that they can consistently perform. Lynnedora must also establish a series of routines and commands that she teaches the whole pack. By doing so, the puppy is spared the confusion of responding to a variety of commands.

"A schedule! We must have a schedule."

Not just a schedule. A schedule that works and can be maintained. Some rules of thumb are necessary to build our schedule around. If at all possible, confinement should be limited to an eight hour maximum. When one member of the family is home all day, or there are responsible children who return from school early, an eight hour maximum should be no problem. Smaller family units, from which all members go out and work, will have a problem. A nearby relative perhaps, or a trustworthy child from the neighborhood can help. Remember, if you bring in reinforcements they must be taught by example to handle the animal exactly as the family handles the animal.

Feed the puppy twice a day. Feed her in the crate if you have one; in a secluded corner, out of traffic flow, if you do not. Throck must not be allowed to drag out the feeding time to suit herself. Give her fifteen minutes, then remove the food. She will quickly learn to finish in that amount of time.

Lynnedora and helpers must also allow time for walking. For the first few days at least, and until the puppy appears well used to the routine, Throck should be walked on lead, even if she has a fenced yard. Take her on a loose lead, coaxing her if necessary. The purpose of these trips is to teach her what the pack leader expects. Use the same routine in the same area and reward success. Gently chastise if she picks up foreign objects, but avoid stern condemnation, especially now.

We also have to fit play periods into the schedule. Life for the baby has to be more than crate to yard to crate. Let her play in the kitchen, where she will likely encounter other pack members and can entice them to play with her. Purchase a gate to block the door. Metal, hard plastic, or plastic coated mesh will do. Plastic mesh soon disappears.

Gates seem to be available in three styles. Some have a notch-ed bar, which you adjust until the sides of the gate squeeze a-gainst the jambs. Some overlap with drop clamps. You squeeze them into place one time, with a wing-nut on a treaded bar. Once in place, the overlapping sides lift and swing open. A third type, which we have only seen in hard plastic, screws into one jamb. By pressing a release, you can then slide it to door width, where it grabs two catches mounted on the opposite jamb. The type you purchase may well depend on how agile you feel. Climbing over, with items in your hands and a puppy on your heels, does not al-ways prove fun or successful. That fact may persuade you to buy one of the easier to open varieties.

Do not ignore signals. At pup's first whimper, whether that precedes your alarm clock or not, bound good naturedly from bed and lead Throck outside. Feed when you return, walk again, and allow fifteen or twenty minutes to romp around the kitchen. Crate! If you are not leaving right away and have time, walk her again before you crate her.

Those of you who do not have to work, or who have helpers, arrange to walk every four hours, give or take. You work all day and have no help? The first minute you return from work, walk, feed, walk, then have a good long play. Walk again and crate her. Keep in mind this process should only take two days to two weeks. Once the message records and Throck's systems adjust, she can take some solo romps in the fenced run and enjoy short-ened play periods with an open-door crate.

"I have to work, but my son will walk her when he comes home from school. Should I put something else in her crate when I leave her?"

Pick a pleasant radio station and leave the radio playing soft-ly. An artificial bone or a hard ball will satisfy her need to chew. Do not leave food. Water, yes! Better yet, fill the pail to overflowing with ice cubes. Be sure to hook the pail to the side of the crate to prevent her accidentally dumping it.

"Not one mistake in a week. Is she housebroken?"

Probably she is!?! Reinforce whenever you can. She may soil your kitchen a time or two in order to get even for long absences. Clean up quickly without ceremony or criticism. If her action gains her no special attention, she will soon abandon that tactic in favor of a better attention getter. If she persists, of course, go back to step one and start over.

Once you feel Throck is solid in her routine, teach a little flexibility. One day each week, walk her to a new destination, by way of a new direction. Throck will soon travel to shows. She cannot take her private restroom with her. Neither can she cross her legs until she returns home. Taking her to different places now and again will teach her something about flexibility, a quality she will need to possess on the show circuit.

There hasn't been a mistake in a week. Wonderful! An animal that has learned to control her eliminations and only relieves herself outside has accomplished a giant step closer to acceptance by the new pack. A happy moment, but not a time to relax. To complete the adjustment, Throck still has much more to learn.

When integrating the puppy,
remember even reluctant members of family.

Pack Tolerance

Often the new pack has multiple members: adults, children, and other animals. One by one, introduce the puppy to each pack member, including kittens, goldfish, and birds. Always remain alert and ready to intervene, limiting responses if necessary. Arrange for daily encounters until both puppy and established members arrive at a truce.

The humans usually want to be too friendly, at least at first. Lynnedora's family anxiously awaited her return with Throck.

There is an instant pack. She only had to remind the family that the puppy needs quality time from them; not just time, but quality time! Two minutes, five, ten. The puppy needs assurance that the new pack exists and welcomes her.

Do not exhaust her. At the first sign of fatigue, put her to rest in her den.

Stairs

Few things cause such panic in puppies as their first encounter with stairs. If you have no stairs at your home, find some nearby and introduce the puppy to them. This obstacle will confront Throck sooner or later. It is better it happens during a training session, when you are ready and able to assist.

Expect the puppy to balk, whether you try taking her up or down first. Do not be surprised if her protest becomes excessive and she tries to pull out of her collar in an attempt to break free and flee the dreaded obstacle. Soothe and comfort her. Sit with her and let her study the foe. When she appears calm, try one step. If you are at the top, support her chest with your hand and ease her down. Rest! Try the next step. Praise each effort. Up is usually easier. First, give her a boost. Then stand above her and coax. Boost again and coax again. It should not take more than three steps. Praise! Praise! Praise!

The first time Throck goes down and up without assistance, praise her lavishly, and add a cookie as a bonus. Then do it again; and a third time. She may still protest a day later. Ignore the protest and start down or up, as the case may be. Throck will follow the leader, reluctantly or otherwise. A few of those episodes and the ordeal will end.

Table Training

While Throck is small enough to lift easily, teach her to accept standing on a table. If your Throck is Cocker size or smaller, she will be judged on a table. Whatever her size, if you value your back, she will be groomed on a table.

Perfect form is not the objective at the start. All you want her to accomplish is a steady stand. Reward her. Make her hold the stand. Reward! Repeat the experience at least three or four times a week. Each time, ask her to hold the pose longer. When she acts as if she accepts the exercise, you then have the option of refining the act. If yours is a breed that is judged on the table, stand on her right. When she lowers her head, press your fingers gently against the throat and lift. The neck should extend fully and arch slightly, supporting a head held high and alert.

While she is standing and behaving, handle her; brush, comb, clip. If she moves, do not scold. Just place her again and start over. Another move should bring a sharp "no" and a more insistent return to stance. If Throck makes it a contest of wills, make sure you win. Grabbing her by the nape of the neck and growling might remind of her mother, her first pack leader, and bring her around.

*Grabbing puppy by nape of neck and growling
may remind her of her mother and discipline her.*

Furniture Usage

You will soon replace the practice table with a grooming table that you can fold and take to shows. As to the rest of the furniture in the house, from beds, to sofas, to chairs, you will have to decide whether Throck will share them with humans or be restricted.

If the furniture is forbidden territory, tell Throck from the very beginning and be consistent in enforcing the rule. You cannot expect Throck to understand that furniture usage is allowed if the humans want to play, but not at other times.

The easier path, or so it seems, is to allow her use of the furniture. We do, but not always without regret. Before you choose this course, remember that Throck will shed, get wet and muddy, and have seasons, if you own a female. Think about your life-style. Will hair on your clothes prove a problem? What about the friends who come to visit? Can your lap handle Throck?

The choice is yours. Left to her own devices, Throck will scramble up at every opportunity. Whichever choice you make, enforce it constantly.

Barking

This is another tough one. How does Throck reason the dif-ference between the praised bark — a warning of an intruder — and the protested bark — an announcement of the garbage men arriving at four in the morning? She can bark a greeting and get a cookie. But barking to protest loneliness brings reprimand. We wish we could offer an easy solution. Continue to praise good barks, ignore marginal barks, and chastise barking for barking's sake.

How to chastise properly is the question. Some ring the dog's nose with their fingers. This does not normally meet with great success. We growl. Yes, growl. The puppy's mother reprimanded her with a growl. If that does not work, roll her on her back and growl. As a last resort, use the conventional squirt gun. A well-washed squeeze bottle will substitute. One inpermissible bark earns one squirt, in the face. Again, be consistent.

Chewing

Protect what you do not want chewed. Hide it, guard it, put a barrier around it. Then hope that you are smarter than Throck. You will win some and lose some over the years.

Substitute something chew-worthy for whatever you prefer to remain unharmed. The nylon products last longest and suit the animals. Never give her anything that can cause a blockage — shoes, meat bones, rawhide.

To be as honest as we can be, the only remedy that seems nearly foolproof is advanced age. Once the adult teeth are in and the puppy gains maturity, the chewing decreases markedly — un-til you let down your guard, that is! If Throck can, she will. The day you get confident and leave something valuable within reach may be the very day Throck relapses. Once she finishes, she will feel guilty. Your verbal attack will make her feel worse. But who is really at fault?

Jumping Up

There is nothing like wearing your favorite outfit and having Throck jump up on it with muddy paws. Unless it's being greeted with a jump when your arms are full of groceries.

The obvious solution is to have the leader stop Throck from jumping up. On the other hand, Throck jumps up to give and receive affection. If you decide to stop her, just gently lift your knee into her chest as she lifts. With smaller animals, use your toe. Do not attempt to hurt her. The idea is to tip her off balance and onto her back. Repeat this treatment every time.

There is a compromise. Instead of using the knee or toe every time, only go that route if you precede the action with the word "no." When affection is the order of the day, allow her up. At other times, warn her away with a "no." Any time she ignores the warning, onto her back she goes.

Reinforcing Den Training

Once the pack is satisfied with the puppy's behavior in all the areas of Den Training, Throck can become a functional member of the family. It will not happen overnight. Remember that you are dealing with a baby.

Also remember that she can relapse into misbehavior. The best way to avoid that happening is to reinforce her in her good behavior, praising and treating her generously. As we said earlier, that puppy's top priority is pleasing you. And if she does backslide? Ignore the first instance, if she shows any sign of remorse. Scold a second offense. A third mistake in the same category signals that the training did not register permanently. Start again.

Never, ever, never — during training or after — strike Throck. That includes the use of hands, leads, or newspapers. You are not training or punishing a huge, wild beast that could terminate your life. This is a friend who wants to please. If she does not please, you have not properly communicated what you expect and how she is to accomplish it.

Finally, we once again remind you that you are training a baby. This newly forming little mind finds the world a wonder, along with everything in it. The attention span is short and distractions are many. Rather than fight the situation, relax and enjoy the distractions with her.

Before leaving Den Training, we need to answer an often asked question about what many consider a part of this early training and adjustment to the den. "Our puppy hates cars and wants to chase them. What can we do?"

We do not incorporate anti-chasing training into our format because we see no need for it. Whether the animal is six months or six years, never take her into danger without a lead. The animals do not understand the dangers. A firecracker, horn, child, another animal − any of these can spook Throck when you least expect it. Unless you are in the car, your home, or a fenced or otherwise confined area, do not allow Throck off lead. Nine times it works and the tenth time your friend is dead. An animal who is properly confined, or is trained to the lead, cannot chase cars. If they cannot chase, it seems a waste of time to train them not to.

SOCIAL TRAINING

The second phase of Throck's training should not commence before she reaches six months. Some people call this phase manners training. Formalized, it is the core of the A.K.C.'s Companion Dog program.

Call it what you will, it is training that requires both handler and animal to employ a serious approach. This phase does teach her to be a companion with manners. More important, this training emphasizes an immediate and positive response to the handler's commands. She is venturing into a dangerous environment now, one she cannot understand without the help of her leader. Failure to respond to the leader's commands in this unfamiliar territory could cost your animal its life.

Many very knowledgeable dog people contend that the purebred who is truly show quality should be pampered and tolerated, much as we pamper and tolerate the star athlete. Obedience training (what we refer to as second phase, or social training), they maintain, can only dull the arrogance and competitive spirit that separates the Best in Show animals from the ones who also participated. They feel the correct sequence is Den Training −

Show Ring Training — Social Training.

Just as vocal are those who cite the animals who have simultaneously competed in obedience and conformation. This group contends that obedience training improves the conformation dog, adding consistency to his other merits. There is no pleasure to be taken from the animal who misuses the pack and is an embarrassment in public, they contend.

We agree and disagree with both sides. We have observed animals who appeared to have lost their competitive edge as a result of social training. We have also known dogs who won both titles, conformation and obedience, after concurrent campaigns. None, however, took a Best in Show along the way.

After much listening and watching, we conclude that the correct approach is determined by the animal in question. Some are subdued by obedience training and others can handle it. There is no doubt in our minds that some of our Champions could have handled both social training and show ring training at the same time. They might well have been able to compete in both areas at the same time. Grab a different collar and lead for each activity and have a go at it.

We are just as certain that there are among our Champions those who could not have handled the dual training and dual competition. Either the social training dampened their enthusiasm for the conformation ring, or the conformation ring would have confused their application of the obedience commands.

To set the record straight, we do not submit our dogs to social training until they finish their conformation championships. That is not to say we recommend that you follow the same course. If you think your animal can handle both, buy two sets of tack and go for it.

Once again, there does appear to be a compromise. Remember that we are only discussing when Throck should receive social training, not if she should receive it. Perhaps the best answer is to teach her the social training exercises without demanding the excellence, or without submitting Throck to the constant repetition that she would have to provide and undergo as a potential competitor in the obedience competitions. If the objectives are the establishment of the trainer as pack leader, the learning of the social graces, and the protection of the animal, who cares if a sit is straight, or a sit stay turns into a down stay.

The snag, of course, comes when and if you decide to compete in the obedience ring at a later date. You will then have to correct and refine less than perfect practices. The choice is yours.

While you are thinking about that, we shall take you out of one controversy and into another. If we proceed on the basis of the compromise mentioned above, we must select an approach. One method advocates training an animal by rewarding the repetition of explained and demonstrated exercises. Mistakes and compliance failures are ignored. Reward success and ignore failure. The second and more often used method is that which relies on commands and penalizes failure to comply by inflicting moderate pain with a choke collar. We have used both methods and prefer the former. Again, the choice is yours.

Please remember that just because a little is good, a lot is not always better. Avoid overtraining. You can increase the length of each session to coincide with your animal's enthusiasm, or fifteen minutes, but not longer.

Keep in mind that the training collar should be removed after each session. At six months of age, she is eligible to compete in conformation. Judges tend to frown on ring-around-the-collar. More important, an animal in a hurry can snag its collar on a protrusion and throttle itself.

Make sure you understand each new lesson before you attempt to teach it. If you are confused, be assured that your animal will also be confused. Throck deserves better. She has a right for her leader to exhibit confidence, consistency, and compassion.

Animals appear to learn best when they are taken to the same place for training. That is not to say that once arrived you cannot vary the routine. We think you should. Go a step further and add in some play once the training ends. Throck can get bored too. Keep her working happily.

As for equipment, there is little you will need beyond what you already own. If you intend to try both obedience and conformation simultaneously, use a narrow leather lead and chain choke for the former, and a nylon lead and collar for conformation. Throck will easily distinguish between the two sets of tack and will understand what is expected when.

About the only other thing you will need is a piece of clothesline, forty to fifty feet long. It will prove invaluable when you teach the stay and recall commands. Make sure you know where your foul weather gear is stored. A day or two of vacation from practice will not hurt either of you, now and then. Five days off will. Consistency means every day, rain or shine.

And one final reminder. Training should be fun for both of you — two friends out on the town. When the trainer gets irritated, quit for the day. When Throck's head droops and the tail stops wagging, quit for the day.

Heeling

Heeling is little more than advanced lead training. When a puppy first goes out on lead, we only hope the puppy moves in the desired direction. As time passes, the puppy learns to go out and back with fewer and fewer distractions.

Heeling expands and refines this exercise. What you want from Throck now is for her to learn to walk with you, sometimes for long distances, moving when you move, turning when you turn, stopping when you stop — all with minimal direction.

Hold one ring of the choke collar in your left hand and one ring in your right, above the left hand. Now lower the chain through the bottom ring, the one in your left hand. As the loop forms, slide it over Throck's head. The ring in your left hand is called the dead ring. The other is the live ring. If you hook your lead to the dead ring, the collar is only a collar. Hook the lead to the live ring and you have a choke collar that tightens on the animal's neck when you tug. Once the collar is on there should only be a three inch slack. More slack requires the trainer to use exaggerated corrections.

Take the lead in your hands and finalize your decision. If you hook to the live ring, you can train using the choke. Hook to the dead ring and you will have to rely on communication and persuasion.

The lead should be held in the right hand, about even with your belt buckle. Allow the lead to droop six to eight inches from the collar, then take up the rest of the slack. The left hand only touches the lead if you are using the choke to correct. In that event, use the left hand to jerk the lead and close the collar.

Shortening up on the lead helps Throck to understand that

her potential for straying has been limited. The tugs of those who prefer a choke collar tell her when she errs. To avoid the discomfort of those tugs, she will soon adjust her behavior. Those of you using the more positive method will use a different approach. What you want is for Throck to accompany you on your walk. What Throck wants is to accompany you on our walk. You are off to a great start.

Throck is a child and life is an adventure. Smells, sounds, movements — everything is new and exciting. It should hardly be surprising if she strays now and again. Talk to her, praise her, keep her moving. If she strays, growl and call her. Reward her renewed attention to you.

Once she understands that straying is not in the program and walks with you apace, throw in some turns — right, left, turn around. Take your time on the left and about turns. Slow motion and exaggeration are in order until she gets the idea. Also, establish a routine with her. Always start with your left foot and stop by bringing the left foot even with the right.

When Throck goes and returns with you without distractions, starts when you start and stops when you stop, she has mastered her first challenge. Smooth turns, executed without tripping or lagging, provide a bonus.

Socializing

Having essentially conquered heeling, the next step is to test her under pressure. There is no time like the present. Shows provide an abundance of noises, smells, and visual distractions. Throck needs to learn to expect almost anything.

Take her for a walk along the main street of the nearest town. On the way home, stop and buy her a dish of vanilla ice cream or a vanilla shake. Make the adventure fun. Two or three days later, take her to town again. This time try to do it when the street is crowded. Weave in and out of pedestrians. If someone wants to give Throck affection, encourage them to do so. Expose her to noises, surprises, and smells. Give her more ice cream.

Throck will soon look forward to your trips. It is time for variety. Take her to shopping malls (if allowed), puppy matches, school yards — anywhere she is likely to encounter people and other animals. When she can handle any new situation without losing her poise, part two is complete.

Sit

This is the command that conformationists fear teaching the most. In formal obedience work, sit is usually taught with heeling. Every time the handler stops, the animal sits beside him. Conformation people fear that animals will also then sit in the conformation ring every time his handler stops. That could be awkward.

Sit

We suggest you teach the sit separately, disassociated from the heeling exercise. Give the command and grab Throck by the collar with the right hand. Lift up on the collar and with the left hand push down on the croup, the last part of the dog's back before the tail. Some prefer to lift on the collar and press their left forearm against the backs of the animal's hind legs. Either will ease the animal into a sit.

Follow the basics of any training step. Command, assist, and reward. Soon you will only have to command and reward.

Down

This is one of the more difficult lessons because the dog hesitates to let even the leader so totally dominate her. Almost always the animal will at first resist.

From a sitting position, command her into a prone position. Facing the same direction she does, reach around her, support her chest, and lift both front legs off the ground. If she protests, be patient. Slowly lower her to the ground or floor. Repeat the assist every time she refuses the command. After many tries she will go down by herself.

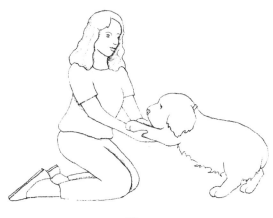

Down

Stay and Recall

In conjunction with the sit and down training, many people teach a second command — stay. As the term suggests, the purpose is to have the dog remain where it is until released by a new command, such as come.

This should be no problem, right? Staying and coming are two of a dog's best things. The problem, unfortunately, is that usually they apply their adeptness in these areas in the exact reverse order of what you might wish, coming when you want them to stay, and staying when you want them to come.

With the animal in a sit or down position and you on the animal's right side, give the command to stay. Reinforce the verbal command with a hand signal — an open palm, two inches in front of the dog's nose is the accepted signal in obedience competitions. Now step out, holding the lead, and turn to face Throck. Allow six inches between you. Stand until you believe her resolve to comply is tested.

After a few such sessions, move back the length of the lead. If the animal attempts to come to you, correct with a sharp "no" and return Throck to her original position. Persist. If you allow the dog a new position, you lose the game. Once stage two is solid, attach that length of clothesline to the lead and retreat twenty feet or so. If she holds, she probably has it.

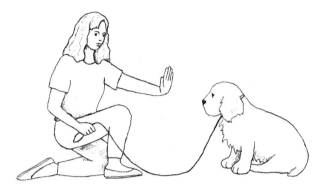

Stay

Now call out the word "come." Obedience people refer to this command as the recall. Use a pleasant tone and body language to make her understand that you welcome her. If she does not get the message, reel her in, hand over hand on the rope. Never let her anticipate. If she breaks a stay and advances without command, return her to her original position. Make her hold a long "stay." Then command her to come. Ask her to sit facing you. Reward her effusively.

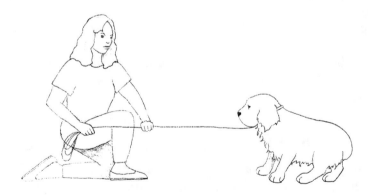

Come

Do not ever use this command to summon Throck for a scolding. She will associate this negative treatment with the command and show reluctance to comply afterwards.

Stand

The stand is easily taught and could be helpful in the conformation ring. While the dog is standing, walk it for two or three strides and then give the command "stand." Obviously the animal was already standing, so you have not accomplished much at this stage. But "stand" in this context means more.

Whether they need it or not, adjust the feet, grasping the leg at the elbow to move the foot. When you are satisfied, give the "stay" and walk six feet away. If Throck moves as much as a foot, scold her and return the foot to the position you indicated. Occasionally have another person go over Throck with his hands while the dog holds its stay. This will begin to accustom Throck to the handling of judges in the ring. If Throck tries to sit, respond immediately with a "no" and an assisted return to position.

"Why can't we just forget the 'sit' and 'down' for now and substitute the 'stand'"?

Because, Lynnedora, Throck cannot hold the stand nearly as long as the other two, no more than you could stand without moving as long as you could sit and lie down. Let's assume a given evening brings company who only tolerate animals. You could crate Throck, but then the crate becomes a prison. Better to include Throck in the group by putting her on a down stay for the evening.

One last time we remind you that the young dog loves you and wants to please you. You are doing her a favor by building her confidence, keeping her safe, and making her socially acceptable. Done with patience and understanding, she will repay your efforts with compliance, friendship, and love.

OTHER TRAINING

We promised two additional training phases. And we intend to keep that promise. Conformation training — the skills of the show ring — are discussed in part two of this volume. Campaign training — the preparation of your animal for the long and arduous circuit necessary to gain national ranking — is addressed in Volume II.

5.

Puppy Health Care

CHOOSING THE VETERINARIAN_____

Beginning the Search

Start with the yellow pages and make a list. Speak to an officer of your local kennel club and make notes next to each name, then pick up the phone and start calling. We can make a personal visit to the survivors later, but first we will shorten the list from your kitchen.

If the call reaches a multi-doctor hospital, be sure to underline that fact in your notes. To their credit, the large hospitals often have the most state-of-the-art equipment and keep it updated with the newest technology. The individual practitioner, unable to afford such elaborate equipment, often has to refer patients with exotic problems to university hospitals.

On the other hand, the single veterinarian office can offer a service that includes continuity and a closer rapport. Many animal owners resent large clinics, which treat them like numbers. Worse, the patient often sees a different doctor each visit. Many owners find that disquieting.

"This may be harder than I thought. Out of five calls, only one impressed me. They sounded very professional. The office runs on an appointment system. I made an appointment since they just took a cancellation. They told me the schedule is very tight because the vet missed three days in the office while he attended a seminar."

It sounds as though he attempts to keep up with the latest information. Give him a plus for that. Did you ask what provision they make to handle emergencies?

"If the answering service cannot reach him, another doctor covers his calls. One or the other is always available."

Visiting the Office

The ride is almost twenty miles. This should be the outer limit for your vet's office, or near it. For routine matters, it is worth the extra time and gas to feel comfortable with the vet, but what happens in the case of an emergency? Twenty miles could take a half hour, and that much delay could be critical.

The clinic is clean inside and out. Score one. Look for something on the wall indicating membership in the American Animal Hospital Association, or a state inspection association. There it hangs, near his degrees. A member of the A.A.H.A.

The receptionist calls for Throckmortana just three minutes after the appointment time. It will not always work that way. Things happen and cause delays. But they do endeavor to remain on schedule. Throckmortana steps on the digital scale and has her weight recorded. She and Lynnedora then follow the young woman into a spotlessly clean examining room.

Five minutes later a smiling man in a clean lab coat joins us, chart in hand. He came prepared, addressing both Lynnedora and Throckmortana by name. To our surprise, he drops to his knees and begs a kiss from Throck before lifting her to the table. That puts everyone at ease, and look at her tail rotate! The comments to his technician indicate an easy working relationship. And yet another surprise, he admits to having never seen a Clumber before and asks for any insights Lynnedora can offer.

While his hands examine, he listens to Lynnedora. We hope she realizes what an unusual occurrence this is. Far too many vets abhor show people and breeders. Now far be it from us to defend every show dog owner and breeder. Obnoxious people appear everywhere. But many, especially the breeders, qualify as experts in their breed. They expect a vet to offer services when necessary, even if those needs arise during off hours. The vet who limits his practice to physicals and shots may well consider the expertise of the client as a threat to his omniscience.

How to Treat the Veterinarian

"What does the vet have a right to expect from me?"

Courtesy, information, and reasonable judgment. Start with courtesy. Make sure he has any previous records pertaining to the animal. Except for emergencies, arrange for an appointment well in advance and keep it. If something prevents you from keeping the appointment, cancel at your earliest opportunity. Again, excepting emergencies, the animal to be examined should be clean. You take a shower before you go to the doctor. And finally, pay promptly.

If the animal is ill, accurate information will help the doctor narrow the possibilities down quickly. At least know the last time Throck ate, how much, and whether there was any dramatic change in water consumption. Has she acted lethargic? Coughed? Vomited? If yes, describe the color and texture of the vomit. Diarrhea? Bloody stool? Now those are not difficult questions. Take a stool sample. Anyone who is half-caring for their animal should answer without hesitation. A show dog owner should do better than that.

Exercise reasonable judgment. No conscientious vet wants you to ignore an emergency, or allow an illness to become an emergency before calling. Neither will he relish two a.m. phone calls because Throck snored.

He has pronounced Throck sound and in good health, the way the dog should be. All we need to do now is teach you the trouble areas to see what you are looking for. Once you understand what should be, you will quickly learn to recognize what should not be. We also, in addition to home health care, want to discuss a comprehensive first aid program with you. When situations arise that compel you to act immediately to save an animal's life, we want you to feel prepared.

THE HOME

"Health care at home. Am I ready?"

If not, you soon will be. Now please do not misunderstand. This section is *not* designed to train you to be a veterinarian. Neither does it pretend to be a substitute for the excellent books on the market, written by vets, describing illnesses in detail and how to remedy them.

Rather, the intention of this section is to help you establish an inspection routine and help you to know what you are looking for. Throck cannot always tell you when something goes wrong. If you recognize good health and proper condition, hopefully during your inspections you will also recognize deviations from the norm — deviations that might warn all is not well.

Inspect Throck at least twice a week. The whole routine, once it is practiced a time or three, only takes a few minutes. If you cannot spare the time, you should not have an animal. Any abnormality should alert, not frighten you. Watch closely for the next day or so. If the problem persists or worsens, call that wonderful vet we found.

Where you choose to inspect the dog will have to be your decision. Consistency is again the important ingredient. Once Throck understands that being led to this place twice each week means a health check, a routine that poses no threat or pain, she will be more anxious to cooperate.

Now remember, you just came from the vet. What you see today is normal and positive. Observe carefully.

Home Inspection of Your Dog

"Here we are, where do I start?"

Anywhere you wish, as long as you follow the same format every time. We keep petroleum jelly and a rectal thermometer in the inspection area and start there. Nothing to it. Dip the thermometer in petroleum jelly. Squeeze your arm around the groin area, where the back legs join the body, so she cannot jump away. Insert the thermometer. After three minutes remove and read. A temperature between 101° F and 102° F is normal.

Anal Glands. As long as you are back there, checking the anal glands next seems logical. There are two, just inside the rectal vent. Leave them alone as long as Throck smells, acts, and moves normally. If, however, her rear opens your sinuses or you witness her licking or biting her rear, dragging or scooting her rear across the ground or floor, showing a hitch in her movement or a reluctance to defecate, run your fingers gently down either side of the anus in search of any swelling. Do not reach inside. If you detect a swelling and/or the abnormal behavior continues, Throck may have to have her anal glands expressed, treated, or removed. All this is best left to the vet.

Coat and Skin. As we mentioned, when selecting a puppy we like to see a glossy coat, full of life. We cannot explain what full of life means, but you will recognize it when you see it. Even better, you will recognize its absence when you do not see it. Ruffle the hair in the opposite direction of the way it grows and search the skin for lumps, scabs, or crust. There should not be any. Pay very close attention to the skin near the root of the tail, armpits, and back of neck. If critters move, Throck probably has fleas. If nothing moves, but you find reddish-brownish-blackish specks, fleas only recently departed. Fleas are a potentially serious problem. We respect their threat enough to devote a separate section to the strategies necessary to combat them further on in the book.

If, during your examination of the coat, you spot insects that appear to be burrowed, head first, into the dog's skin, it is undoubtedly a tick. With the ever increasing incidence of Lyme disease — carried by certain ticks — consider these little guys to be double trouble. In removing them, wear gloves since the blood of certain varieties of ticks can transmit to humans both Lyme disease and Rocky Mountain Spotted Fever. Swab the area around the tick with alcohol, which should help the tick to withdraw its hold. Using tweezers, dig the tick out of the dog's skin. Do *not* leave any part of the tick in the skin of the dog. Sometimes the tick breaks in half or the head remains in the skin and this can be dangerous too, since it can lead to infection. Ticks do not die easily, and are best disposed of by flushing down the toilet.

Feet and Nails. For some reason, the feet and nails are too often overlooked as a source of problems, incapacitating problems, by owners. If the animal is standing on a flat surface and his nails touch the ground, the nails are too long. If you leave them that way the toes will splay, the feet will spread, and the animal eventually will go lame. Check the grooming section for a discussion of nail clips and the correct method of cutting.

Keep those feet in prime condition at all times. First clip excess hair and any mats from between the pads and between the toes. Then look for cuts or abrasions, any stones, mud clots, or other foreign bodies that might lodge between pads. Animals living in snow areas have extra problems with ice chunks and salt. If you must walk your friend in areas where the municipality uses salt, wash and dry the feet after each winter walk. Antiseptic ointment between the toes will protect against rash. One of the things you do not want to encounter is an inflamed interdigital cyst, or growth between the toes. If spotted early, these cysts can some times be treated by soaking the area in Epsom salts three or more times a day for five minutes. Do not wait long. We have seen them balloon from bulge to ping-pong ball in a hurry. If there is no improvement in a week, go to the vet.

Mouth. You reached the other end. After a few more practice sessions, the journey will take much less time without sacrificing thoroughness. We still want to see those shining white teeth in pink gums. Dry dog food and chew bones prevent plaque build up. If the breath smells bad and the teeth look yellow, mix some salt and baking soda together and apply with a cloth or soft brush. Do not forget to rinse. If the breath continues to smell bad, the gums bleed, or the teeth feel loose you know who to call.

Nose. No problem here. We still prefer to find the nose cool and moist, but do not worry excessively if it is warm and dry. A discharge from the nose does concern us, especially if it is accompanied by sneezing.

Eyes. The eyes should be clear and bright. Watch for excessive tearing, blinking, and mucous. Wipe any deposits from the corners of eyes with a moist tissue. Be concerned enough to pick up the phone if the eyes react to normal light, display cloudy corneas, or reveal different size pupils.

Ears. Smell them. If they smell foul, flatten them against the head and swab them out with a cotton ball soaked in mineral or baby oil. Clean only what you can see. Pull the ear back and let the oil run down. Massage the base of the ear and gently mop out. Allow the animal to shake its head and mop again. If the foul smell persists, or Throck keeps pawing at or shaking her head, vet, here we come.

Administering Medication

Pour liquid medications into the pocket between the lip and teeth, then close the lips. Pills present increased difficulties. Most vets suggest making the dog sit, open the mouth with the nose pointed toward the ceiling, drop the pills to the back of the throat, close the mouth, and massage the throat to promote swallowing. This works and reduces the chances of having fingers nipped. We stuff the pills in the little pocket behind the teeth, next to where the tongue roots. Dogs rarely spit them back from there. We have yet to be bitten, but . . .

Eye drops go directly into the eye. Hold the lids open with the thumb and finger of one hand and apply drops with the other. If you must treat the eye with an ointment rather than drops, pull down only the lower lid and apply the ointment to the inside of the lid.

EMERGENCIES AND FIRST AID

The First Aid Kit

The choice of container to act as the actual kit we can leave up to you. We suggest that you make it lightweight and waterproof, and it does not have to be metal with a red cross symbol. A great choice will hold all of the items mentioned and preserve them in a ready-to-use condition. The perfect choice loads and unloads easily, prompting you to take it every time.

The list of items below is a list of the things that should appear in your kit. We invite you, on your next visit, to check this list with your vet. If he objects, or prefers something else, substitute. The vet is the professional and your approach should be consistent. Until then, we recommend the following:

Alcohol, rubbing
Ammonia, aromatic spirits
Blanket
Boric acid
Brandy
Buffered aspirin
Calamine lotion
Camphorated oil
Charcoal, activated
Cotton, absorbent
Cotton balls
Cotton swabs
Disinfectant, broad base
Enema bag
Epsom salts
Gauze bandage — 1" and ½"
Hydrogen peroxide
Iodine
Lead and choker, extra set
Mercurochrome™
Milk of magnesia tablets
Muzzle-belt, pantyhose, nylon lead
Mustard, dry

Nail clippers
Newspapers
Paregoric
Pepto Bismol™ tablets
Petroleum jelly
Phisohex
Plastic bags and/or a hot/cold water
   bottle
Rectal thermometer
Rubber gloves
Scissors, regular and blunt
Shock juice (four tblsps of sugar to
   one pint of water)
Sponge
Spoon, wooden
Stretcher board
Styptic powder
Suppositories
Talcum, medicated
Tape, adhesive, non-stick
Tourniquet
Towels, small and large

That sounds like a lot. Probably it is, but assemble it all. And do not cheat. An extra lead in the tack box and pantyhose in the suitcase are not the same as everything in one place, ready for an emergency. Pray that the whole thing is a waste of money and never gets used.

"I feel like I'm a vet, with all this."

As the pack leader you will rise to the occasion if Throck is seriously injured or impaired. You will keep her alive until she reaches professional help, without worsening Throck's condition.

Go to a copy place and make copies of this section. Show the information to your vet. If there are no objections to the information, put the copies in your kit for quick reference. Memories often fail under the pressures of an emergency.

Before we discuss what to do and when to do it, let us use this opportunity to remind you that a little common sense can avoid problems, which is a whole lot better than sustaining life with first aid. Review the lists we covered under puppyproofing; enemies have a way of sneaking in when the guard is down or complacent. Do not take Throck out of confined areas off-lead. Open windows to lower vehicle temperatures, but do not open them too far. Make sure the crate and fence latches are correctly in place. Even with a double tether, do not have animals ride in the bed of pick-up trucks. The list goes on. A child grows and eventually reasons. Throck will always depend on you.

Several injuries can cause shock. Before you attempt to assist an animal in shock, protect yourself against the possibility of biting with a muzzle, a belt, pantyhose, or gauze. Tie the mouth shut between the nose and the rear of the jaw. Circle the nose one more time and tie behind the ears. Cover the animal with the blanket from your kit and keep him warm. If the animal in unconscious or semi-conscious, about all you can do is get him to a vet. If he is conscious, try a little shock juice or brandy, even coffee, tea, or warm broth. If he will take any, it will provide a heart stimulant.

The time may come when you will need to apply artificial respiration or Cardio-Pulmonary Resuscitation. It is tough to do without inserting a tube, but worth a try when all else fails. Put the animal on his right side and massage behind the left armpit with the heel of your hand. Press chest rapidly, at the rate of 120 times per minute. If this is not effective, stop occasionally, clear the dog's mouth, be sure the mouth is closed so that no air escapes through there, and cover his nose with your mouth. Breathe gently into the nose for three seconds. Massage.

On occasion, you may also have to use the Heimlich maneuver, not easily done with some of the big dogs. Essentially it's performed about the same as on a human. From the back, hug under the last rib and press sharply upward. Repeat quick, sharp squeezes until the object dislodges. It would seem prudent to give some advance thought as to how to accomplish that with your animal. A Mastiff is a problem. A Papillon, in its tiny way, could present a different, yet equally difficult, problem.

Enough for the generalities and on to the specifics. Do not speed read just because you will have this information in your kit. Read slowly and think each procedure through carefully, now, while you are relaxed and have the time. Teach yourself now so that you will only have to review when under pressure. Remember, with the possible exceptions of choking and drowning, the end result is always the vet's office.

Treating Injuries

Abdominal Injury. Wrap body to reduce deep breathing and keep animal warm to prevent shock.

Bloat. An abdominal obstruction. Throck may evidence repeated swallowing, gagging, abdominal distention, and labored breathing. Comfort him and hurry.

Burns. First, second, third degree, and electrical. A first degree burn is the superficial one. The hairs remain firmly attached, and the tender, inflamed skin may blister. Always wash your hand before touching affected area. Apply ice water pack.

Both epidermis and dermis are damaged in second degree burns. Hair will appear badly singed, but remains intact. Fluid will accumulate under the skin. The animal may well go into shock. If hair falls out and injured areas ooze, the burn is probably third degree. There will be little evidence of pain, but shock is probable. With second and third degree injuries, do everything possible to avoid infection. Cover wound with ice water-soaked gauze and transport to vet.

Electrical burns can be dangerous to the owner also. Detach

power source, or use rubber gloves and wood to separate the electrical line from animal. Labored breathing and irregular heartbeat signal that lungs are filling. Comfort the animal and transport quickly.

Choking. If you can see the culprit, gently dislodge it, unless it is string. In that case the other end may already be well into the intestines. If you cannot see the object, try the Heimlich. Should all emergency treatment prove futile and breathing continues to be a struggle, assist with artificial respiration as you travel to the vet.

Constipation. This really concerns professional handlers, because they do not want Throck to develop the urge in the ring. Try a teaspoon of milk of magnesia, or one milk of magnesia tablet per five pounds of dog, up to eight teaspoons.

Diarrhea. Something as simple as a change of water can cause it. But its persistence can be extremely debilitating. For each ten pounds of dog, give one tablet of Pepto Bismol™. Follow it with some bland food: rice, macaroni, or lean meat. If condition persists, or goes away and returns in a few days, have your vet analyze a stool sample.

Dislocations. This occurs when the bone is displaced from the joint. The animal will usually restrict his own movement, but the joint may swell and appear deformed. Have the vet check to make sure bone and joint have returned to the proper alignment.

Drowning. Much to many people's surprise, dogs do drown. Hold them upside down to drain water, then administer artificial respiration. When animal starts to breathe, assume it is in shock and treat accordingly.

Eye injuries. These come in various shapes and sizes. The most common derive from foreign bodies, abrasions, and insect bites. Flush these injuries out with clean, cold water. A warm water-soaked pad will reduce swelling.

More jarring to the uninitiated is seeing an animal with a proptosed eyeball — an eyeball out of the socket. First settle your stomach, then wrap the eye with moist gauze to prevent drying.

Corneal lacerations also occur. Do not panic. Cover with a gauze pad to prevent use and get her to the vet.

Fractures. These come in three varieties. A fracture breaks the bone. If the crack does not displace the bone from its original po sition, the fracture is incomplete. A simple-complete fracture displaces, but not enough to pierce the skin. When the bone is broken, displaced, and piercing the skin, the fracture is compound-complete. Swelling and pain are usually localized around the area of fracture, while the skin over the break often displays a blotchy hemorrhage.

Before you do anything else, muzzle the animal. Make sure that there is breathing, any bleeding is controlled, and the animal is as quiet as possible. If the injury is a compound-complete fracture to the leg, first cover area with sterile pad and secure with bandage. Pad leg with dish towels, then roll newspaper to make a splint. Making sure the splint is long enough to extend past the fractured bone's natural joints on both ends and secure the splint with half-inch bandage. Tie firmly, without shutting off circulation.

Do not allow animal to walk. Use your board or blanket as a stretcher. Spinal fractures increase the danger to the animal. There is not much you can do, except immobilize and transport. Without bending the neck or back in any way, slide the injured animal onto the stretcher board, pulling slowly on the loose skin of the back and neck. If legs are not injured and conditions prevent pulling the animal back first, pull by the legs, keeping them perpendicular to the back.

While transporting, prop the stretcher so that the head is slightly lower. Check breathing regularly. If it stops, remove the muzzle, clear any mucus, and administer artificial respiration.

Frostbite. If Throck has been out for extended periods in dangerous temperatures, check her ears, tail, and toes for red and swollen skin. Sponge areas with warm, 110° F water, then pat dry. If the skin flakes and peels, cover area with petroleum jelly.

Hemorrhage. If blood is spurting and the wound is on a leg, apply a tourniquet. Place it between the wound and the heart, loosening it every eight to twelve minutes. Wounds on the body are more difficult. Apply direct pressure to the wound with the towel or your hand. If necessary to control the bleeding, maintain that pressure all the way to the vet's.

Hyperthermia. Are heavy panting, red gums, and slobbering evident? Trouble!! Whether competing or shut in a car, an animal showing these symptoms is in big trouble. Heart rate may reach

180°, temperature 107° F, combined with vomiting and diarrhea, followed by collapse.

This is neither the time to panic, flagellate yourself for stupidity, or dally. Move the animal to a shaded or air-conditioned area. Cool him down. Submerge him to the neck in cold water, or apply rubbing alcohol to stomach and groin area. Rub legs to stimulate circulation. Check temperature every ten minutes. Do not be satisfied until you have it below 103° F. Also monitor the gums; gray means "get me to the vet as fast as you can."

Early in our show experience, we saw an animal go down from the heat. It was not our dog, but the episode convinced us that showing in excessive heat was not worth the risk. We monitor very closely on warm days. When an animal does go down, the immediate problem is locating cold water or ice. If you carry a cooler, load it with as much ice as possible. Another method is filling plastic containers with drinking water and freezing them into blocks. We might add that show committees would do well to assure an adequate supply of ice at any warm weather show.

Hypothermia. A less common occurrence, but equally life threatening. A temperature check shows 88° F. You place your fingertips on the inside of the left rear thigh and detect a weak, almost absent, pulse. Big trouble again. A dog cannot shiver with a temperature below 90° F. 75° F can be fatal.

Now we have to get the temperature up. Use a warm water bath, warm pack on stomach, hair dryer, or vigorous rubbing. If the animal will drink, give it some shock juice. When you transport, make sure you wrap him in a blanket.

Insect bites, bee stings, allergies. These are not at all uncommon in spring to autumn. If a bite or sting swells, apply ice packs and a baking soda paste. Stings and allergies can cause anaphylactic reactions — wheezing, choking, and fainting. Treat these symptoms just as you would shock. Be prepared to give CPR if throat swells and breathing stops.

Poison. Bloody diarrhea, acute bleeding from mouth or genitals, or convulsions can signal poisoning. By the time you see symptoms, probably only a precise antidote will save the animal. Up to that time, there may be some alternatives. If at all possible, find the culprit. It is difficult to calculate an antidote without a clue. If you are lucky, you will find the container.

If the container suggests an antidote, if the animal is comatose, if two hours have passed since the ingestion, or if you are without container and have reduced the possibilities to an acid, solvent, or petroleum product, pack him up and get to the vet. If, however, the animal is still alert and the ingestion was recent, either the container and/or vet may recommend inducing vomiting. Hydrogen peroxide in a 3% solution will accomplish that. We prefer dry mustard — one teaspoon to a quart of warm water.

Punctures. Danger depends, of course, on the cause, size, and depth of the puncture. Unless it is something beyond the garden variety tooth puncture, just fill it with hydrogen peroxide, 3%. For more extreme punctures, you may have several things to treat. The most obvious would be hemorrhage and shock.

Sprains. When joint-supporting ligaments stretch or tear, Throck has a sprain. Somehow it usually happens for no apparent reason, a half hour before competition. There is usually swelling and voluntary restriction of movement. Many handlers try to mask the pain with pain killers and compete the dog. You can do that and probably get away with it. A better idea is withdrawing from competition and applying a towel-wrapped bag of crushed ice for five or ten minutes every two hours.

6.

Puppy Conditioning

GROOMING

You must understand that every breed has its own grooming and trimming do's and don'ts, best learned from the breeder. What we intend to do here is to provide an overview to prepare you for grooming as part of conditioning your friend. In all cases we have tried to consider the fact that you will soon be grooming for competition. Whenever possible, we want you to avoid duplication and waste in purchasing.

Shop around before buying supplies and equipment. Cheap prices often mean cheap products soon to be replaced. Expensive, by comparison, could mean top-of-the-line, last-forever products. The scenario to avoid — expensive price, cheap product.

It is not necessary to build a grooming room for one dog, but you should try to work in the same place. An ideal location has an easy-to-clean floor and good lighting from above and behind.

With every purchase, remind yourself that you must take your show on the road. It makes a difference. Your tack box, for instance, that large container in which you keep your supplies and much of your equipment, can be wood or metal, poorly or well constructed, plain or decorative, small or large.

Basic Supplies

Brushes. Start with a natural bristle brush. You want tufts of bristles in graduated lengths. The tufts should be set in a base of cushioned rubber, double backed.

Add a pin brush. Again, look for a cushioned rubber base, double backed, but this time holding stainless or chrome-plated pins with rounded heads. Run your thumb through the pins several times, or until you are satisfied the pins are flexible.

Many people with smooth-coated breeds use the rubber brush.

It is much the same as the natural bristle, except the bristles are soft rubber.

Combs. You will use the comb after brushing to arrange the hair and untangle. For a silky haired dog, a fine comb is recommended; average coats require a medium one; coarse for dense coats. Throck will require a medium, but the half-medium, half-fine combs prove very useful. Two stripping combs. They resemble a regular comb with one edge serrated. Buy a fine one for heads, medium or coarse for bodies.

Clippers. Plug-ins are less expensive but difficult to use at a show without electrical outlets available. If you only use them for small jobs, you can substitute with scissors. Heavy users should spend more and buy the cordless rechargeables. Save some of that money by using your clippers as often as possible on clean hair only. Dirty hair dulls blades and blades cost money.

Conditioners. There are lots to choose from. Apparently some work better for a given breed than others. Then, too, there can be specific problems. Repeated tangling, for example. Try one with antiseptics added. Coat is dull? Oils add luster. Lifeless? Conditioners with polypeptide proteins supposedly add body. Often times a balanced conditioner is all you will ever need. Pick up the phone and check with your breeder.

Crate tops. Offering a rubber or vinyl surface, these tops cover a crate and provide a grooming surface on which you can place the dog. Some crates come with permanent tops. They are wonderful for inside shows, where space is at a minimum. But they can also be tough on the back of a tall person. Our major objection is that there is no way of restraining the animal during grooming. A distracted moment and Throck can be off to the races.

Douche powder. You'll be happy you have this powder if Throck turns up a skunk. Bathe her in Massengill and water. No douche powder? Use tomato juice.

Forceps. 5½" Kelly forceps are great for ear hair.

Grooming table. Again, there are choices — round, rectangle, oval; 24" X 36", 18" X 30", 24" X 42". All that we have seen are 30" or 34" high, with 6" to 10" leg extenders available. Consider both your size and the adult size of your puppy. Make sure the table has a non-slip rubber top and provision for an adjustable post and loop, the restraining device. (This is a metal post that bends into a right angle. A loop hangs from the end of the section that runs parallel to the table. Height is adjusted by loosening the vise or screw clamp and raising or lowering the vertical post.)

One thing we should mention about the restraining device; a looped dog is not nailed to the table. If he jumps, with luck he will pull the table over with him. The alternative is hanging himself. When you have an animal on the table, keep yourself there with him. A few seconds lapse can bring a terrible result.

Avoid, if you can, tables that have a place for the arm within the surface area of the table. We have one and the metal clamp that holds the post is always in the way. It holds the post more securely than some of the clamp-ons, but it certainly offsets that advantage with inconvenience.

Many of the new tables also come equipped with large wheels. When the table is collapsed, it can then serve as a come-along, on which you can pile crates, tack boxes, etc. Little wheels bog down in mud. If you prefer a table with the wheels option over a wheelless table and separate come-along, make sure the wheels are three to four inches in diameter.

Hound glove. This is a mitt equipped with bristles — wire, sisal, horsehair, or fiber. Many people prefer them to brushes.

Knives. Depending on your breed, we suggest two or three. Everyone should have a common jackknife in the box for any number of uses. Most everyone will also benefit from the inclusion of a stripping knife — a single blade with one serrated edge. There is a knife with two serrated blades called the undercoat knife. Owners of breeds with heavy undercoats use these to card the dead wool from the undercoat.

Mat splitters. Shaped like a rake, the blades have one sharp edge and blunt ends. They open the mats that the lighter weight picks cannot.

Misters. Simple plastic bottles with squeeze nozzles. You will want a dozen, ultimately, for shampoos, conditioners, and plain water. Ones too tall can be a problem when you try to close the tack box. All the same size and color gets confusing.

Nail clippers. Select from several types on the market. You will find people who prefer whichever you choose. Just make sure your choice has two cutting edges.

Scissors. One pair will do. Buy quality scissors and shears. In this case, you want something five inches long, with blunt tips, to trim feet.

Scissor pliers. A handy gadget used to adjust tensions.

Shampoos. There are lots of choices. You should purchase a tearless shampoo, with a pH around 7.5, and also a waterless shampoo.

Shears. We repeat, buy the best you can afford. You want something that will last for years, hold an edge, resharpen easily, and feel comfortable in your hand. Stainless shears hold an edge as long as carbon steel and resist rust. Plain grounds give a smoother cut than serrated. We suggest something in the 7" to 8½" range.

You also need thinning shears of equal quality. Forty-four or forty-six teeth work well, with an extra fine single edge. Use them to neaten, thin, or blend, cutting against or with the hair. Never cut across the coat.

While we are on the subject of shears, let's take a moment to discuss care. Even a superior product can deteriorate under misuse. Use them only to cut hair. Case and store them as soon as you finish, because rain showers can be sneaky. Lubricate them with oil before each storage, and store with a chalk block that will absorb moisture.

Slicker. A slicker is really another type of brush with two gauges of wire bristles. They come in three sizes – small through large. Great for removing shedding hair and last minute touch-ups. No one should be without a slicker.

Tack box. Quality construction and appropriate size are the important considerations. Look for a box that is durable, water repellent, flexible, well-hinged, with clasps that stay closed, and sturdy carrying-handle assembly. Most have a section in the cover for storing leads, drawers or trays, and an open section for bottles. A final consideration: in the frenzy of competition, the inside often becomes a disaster. Buy something that cleans easily.

Tubs. For now, just think about them, and keep your eyes open. You can struggle along with the sink or family tub. Remember Throck is quick and impulsive. Stepping away for a moment to pick up the phone is all it takes for a disaster. Apartment dwellers and renters will likely never purchase a tub for the grooming area.

Homeowners, especially those with multiple animals, will strongly consider one. Breeders almost require one. A tub needs to be in a place that is easy to enter and exit and easily cleaned. Remember to have it at a height convenient to the washer.

Brushing

What a break that an activity so beneficial to Throck is so easily accomplished! With a few strokes of a brush we can remove dirt and dead hair. At the same time, the brush spreads the natural oils and stimulates new hair growth. Activating those oil glands is especially important before each shampoo.

First, mist the coat with diluted conditioner, then brush with long strokes. If your Throck has a smooth coat, use the pin brush or hound glove against the hair, tail to head. Then go with the hair and down the legs. Double coat? Work from skin outward. Brush long haired dogs against the grain and short haired dogs with the grain. Very long haired varieties brush more easily if you lay them on their side and brush away from the parts. Watch for tangles and mats, especially behind the ears, and remove immediately before a hot spot develops.

Bathing

What can be difficult about bathing? Nothing much. After all, in theory you need only bathe dogs with heavy undercoats twice a year, silky coats once. Between baths, use waterless shampoo.

So much for theories. Show dogs require a separate set of theories. We feel more comfortable saying that Throck should be bathed as often as necessary. Starting as a puppy, when necessary may be often, consider the bathing routine part of her training. Teach her to stand and accept. You will not have the time, energy, or patience to battle her every time she bathes. You taught her the stand-stay, now use it.

Throck is ready. You brushed her to stimulate the oil glands, removed the mats, checked the water to make sure it's warm, and put the tearless shampoo within easy reach. Stand her where she needs to be and reassure her. Make it fun if you can, with lots of touching, praise, and soothing chatter. Rinse her first, slowly from rear to front. If she tries to bolt, stand her again. Do not pamper. If she realizes misbehavior brings extra affection, she will not hesitate to use it again.

Apply the pH 7.5 shampoo, working back to front. Your hand will do; a sponge works well. If you have a long haired breed, squeezing the shampoo through the hair. Rinse well. The correct pH shampoo should rinse out easily. Make sure you get it all.

We use a four application method: shampoo twice, cream rinse to offset static, then conditioner. Pat dry. Do not rub.

There are those special occasions when Throck challenges you with a special problem, such as a coat sporting chewing gum or smelling of feces. No need to panic. For every action there is a proper reaction. All we have to do is find it. Some proper reactions we discovered through the years include icing the chewing gum, and the douche powder works well against feces smell. Try liquid tangle remover or baby oil on those intricate tangles. Wait an hour, then brush. Tar? Use salad oil or dishwashing liquid. A soft toothbrush works wonders on difficult stains.

"What if Throck is shedding?"

A bath will hurry the process. Animals who live in the house, under artificial light and in the heat, seem to shed more than those who spend a lot of time outside.

"Do I ever wash the eyes?"

You probably will, each time, accidentally. That is why you use tearless shampoo. An additional wash with boric acid solution on occasion cannot hurt.

In drying, some like it hot and others like it cool. The breed you have, or more specifically the coat texture of that breed, usually dictates whether or not you have a choice.

For Throck, we prefer the cool air blower that simply removes the excess water. The animal remains damp and air dries in the crate. The alternative, the hot air blower, evaporates the excess water and finishes drying the dog. Without a doubt, most people use this second method. Blow dry lotion helps the coat to maintain natural oils in the presence of heat. If the coat frizzes, finishing sprays are available.

Many of the owners of breeds with medium length coats, or coats that should stand away from the body, prefer to fluff dry. Use a natural-bristle pin brush or a fine-wire slicker in combination with your dryer.

Those of you who must layer-dry win both our admiration

for your patience and our sympathy for your ordeal. Always start with the right side. Save the show side for last. One little thing to remember. When you switch sides, replace the damp towel on which the wet dog was lying with a dry one to receive the dry side of the animal. When Throck dries, whether artificially or naturally, comb him one last time. It helps the hair distribute evenly.

Trimming

Much of the trimming is dictated by the standards for your particular breed. There are considerations for every breed.

Feet that stay well trimmed track in far less mud. If you use electric clippers, remember that they get hot. A good scissor cut is made with the scissors flat against the hair. If the hair slides towards the points while cutting, have the scissors sharpened.

Toenails need cutting. Many people hate this task. It is really quite easy, if approached correctly and often. Locate the quick, the line of different color extending from the foot toward the end of the nail. Where it ends, you stop cutting.

Use cutters with two cutting edges and work from the end of nail towards the quick. Stop just before you reach the quick. Take only small pieces at a time. A yelp, jerk, and blood announce you went too far. Try to avoid this last, for both your sakes. If it happens, it will not be the last time. Stop the bleeding with antiseptic powder or a wet tea bag, and move to the next nail. One consolation, each time you cut, the quick retreats before the next time.

One other trouble area is ear hair! If the hair inside the ear thickens to the point that air flow is restricted, it has to go. Pluck the crop thin with your forceps.

FLEAS

Some years, especially on the show circuit, you and Throck will encounter fleas. Save your money! From what we observe, flea collars offer little protection. As soon as you get her home, use a flea shampoo, a sharp eye, and quick fingers to kill fleas. Do not expect the shampoo to provide much in the way of residual protection. You should also purchase an implement called an English flea comb. The closely-spaced teeth search the hair thoroughly and bring fleas to the surface.

Then there are years when you and Throck will encounter flea infestations and bring them home. What a mess! Dogs scratching and biting themselves bald; people covered with bites; rugs, chairs, even beds housing the vicious enemies.

First, understand the enemy. There are four phases in the life-cycle of a flea: egg, larva, pupa, and adult. Depending on variety, egg to adult requires three weeks to eight months. To give you an idea of how tough the enemy is, adult females can go a year or more without food and still lay eggs every day. Now that's tough!

Spray the inside of your vehicle, every crack and crevice, with a pyrethrin spray for adults and methoprene for larvae. While the car airs out, bathe Throck. Protect her eyes with a dab of ointment in each, then bathe her again with flea dip, to which you add oil. Pat her dry, then allow her to finish naturally on a towel in the car, with the windows all cracked for good ventilation.

Spray the yard with a 5% carbamate dust (Sevin), or a malathion-methoprene combination. We also like plain Clorox®, diluted 12:1.

Move to the house and evacuate the family to the vehicle. Most pet supply places sell fog bombs. These devices come with estimated coverage specifications. Follow them closely and buy enough for cellar to attic coverage. Shut windows and doors, open closets and drawers and bed covers. Activate the bombs, the one closest to the door last. Take Throck and the family for a two hour lunch and ride.

As soon as you return, have the family cushion the crate and any outside sleeping area with cedar shavings. While they are busy with that, take a new sweeper bag and put a handful of moth crystals in it before attaching it to the cleaner. Sweep everything you can reach. Burn the bag outside, if allowed. Sweep every day with crystals.

Keep cedar shavings about, spray the yard every two weeks, vacuum every day. Flea comb at least daily. Conditions should improve to tolerable immediately. Total victory will prove elusive.

KEEPING IN SHAPE

You and Throck are preparing to participate in a sport, a sometimes physically demanding sport. She must represent her breed as well as she is able. As her handler, you must allow her to do so. Enhance her performance if possible; never detract. As her teammate, we leave it up to you to decide whose fat and muscle tone need attention.

Throck cannot monitor her diet and weight the way you do. We worked hard to trudge through the nutritional morass and locate the most beneficial food product. Quality you have, so adjust the quantity. When she works hard, allow her a larger ration. Lying around making shadows requires short ration.

"Sounds simple enough."

That's because it represents only one-half the equation. We spell the other half of the equation — exercise.

"Exercise! But that's the reason we built a run, so Throck could exercise herself."

As we remember, Lynnedora, the justification for the run contained qualifiers you are forgetting to mention. The run allows the dog to exercise herself alone on inclement days, or in days of human illness. Because she has a run does not mean she can only exercise there. Besides, Throck exercising herself would do little for your muscle tone.

Tired times provide an opportunity to activate the reserves. The children want involvement with Throck. Let them go out to the run and join her in catch, monkey-in-the-middle, or races. Explain to them how much they help their dog and you.

At times when you feel more energetic, at twilight or with the dawn, you and your husband take her out for a jaunt. A quarter mile, a half mile. Work up to a mile. Walk, jog, stretch the humans a bit, push them a little farther.

Fortunately for you, we now live in the age of the retractable leads, feet and feet and feet long. Jog where there are open spaces — fields, meadows, parking areas. Give Throck the freedom to reel out and in as often as she wants. In the same journey, she will travel ten times the distance you travel without taxing your energy in the least.

ENJOYING YOUR PUPPY

"Is it too soon to play?"

It is never too soon for a puppy to play. From early on, she plays with her litter mates. Why not her new pack mates? In the house or out, she will love tag, fetch, tug-of-war. She will give it everything she has, in an effort to please, out of a desire to belong. The people will have to take responsibility for limiting the scope and longevity of the game.

Especially with the large breeds, limit jumping. The parts are not fully formed and strengthened. Watch for fatigue; Throck's fatigue. If you only have a minute or so, the difficulty will arise when you try to convince her the game is over. Playing many short games will help her understand.

One more caution. When playing, do not praise and encourage behavior that you will not accept at other times. Furniture usage, for example. You will only confuse her if you allow her in the rocker while playing, then forbid her on every other occasion. You will be allowing her to link the unacceptable behavior with fun, then reprimanding her. At least, it is inconsistent; at most confusing.

PHOTOGRAPHING YOUR DOG

"Are photos necessary, or optional?"

From our point of view, both. Take memories for instance; are they optional or necessary? One of the sadnesses of having a pet for a friend is that, in human terms, the friendship proves brief. Ten years, twelve. And then, there are only memories to fill the empty place.

We vote for quality memories: puppy, adult, senior; casual, posed, moving, head study. Accumulate as many memories as you can. Also, you have informal obligations. If the breeder lives across country, pictures or slides provide the only visual record of the puppy's development and the success of the breeder's program. And you may well have contracted to breed at least once. A distant potential buyer will want to see a picture of Throck and the puppies. If you continue to breed, a prospect we shall consider seriously in Volume II, the reasons for having a good camera and a basic understanding of how to use it multiply.

Remember how we compared three generations of Throck's family looking for genetic trends? It seems only fair that you contribute to that all too shallow informational pool as an aid to those who come after.

Decent photography is not that difficult, and after the initial outlay, not that expensive. If you can only afford an inexpensive camera, use that. There are several reasonably priced 35mm cameras on the market.

Candid shots always make the best photos; at least those that appear candid. Fill as much of the picture as you can with the subject, always keeping her just off dead center.

Whether your photos are memory, obligation, or analysis, this year, next year, or twenty years from now, you will want to have them. Store those prints and slides in a cardboard box or in a cabinet drawer if you can't find time for a photo album. You will never regret your collection.

REMEMBER YOUR DOG

"I've been so busy buying and learning that I feel I have neglected Throck. That concerns me. Most of all, I want Throck and the family to come out of this best friends."

On behalf of your breeders, we thank you for that. If her former owners had any doubts about the sale, those words dissolved them.

Please stand by your convictions. We see show dog owners wander from their true intent all the time. They busy themselves talking, kennel clubbing, and national clubbing. One day they look down at the animal who is supposed to be the focus of all this effort and wonder who he is. How terribly much they miss.

We have had a busy few weeks together, Lynnedora; preparing, selecting, buying, training, bonding. Maybe we've been too busy. Take a month or two to walk and talk with Throck, play with her and cuddle her, give love and accept it. Make certain to include the whole family.

Then have everyone take a very deep breath. Soon it will be Showtime.

II

The Sport of Dog Showing

7.

A Moment for Nostalgia

Sometimes it seems like only yesterday that we became interested in purebred dogs. Years pass, memories pile on memories, chronological order wallows in confusion. These are some of the problems with growing old. That is probably why it seems like only yesterday that we started raising purebred dogs.

When we walk through a yard teeming with Clumbers and Shepherds of various ages, reach down to pat the older ones sleeping around the writing table, and survey the ribbons, trophies, and finishing pictures that adorn the walls, we must rule out yesterday. There are so many victories and defeats, friends past and present, joys and heartaches, lessons learned the hard way. All of that could not have happened since yesterday.

DECIDING TO OWN A DOG_____

Many yesterdays ago, we returned to the mainland, after living several years in Puerto Rico. We thought it kinder to leave our eight horses and six mutts in good homes on the island rather than subject them to the trauma of Pennsylvania, the land of erratic weather and uncertain future. It was an unpleasant interval for us. Only Sylvester, our Russian Blue cat born on the mainland, traveled with us.

Our first stop was a rented duplex; no pets allowed. Sylvester stayed with relatives. Next we moved to a rented house, no pets allowed. Sylvester remained with relatives. Neither of those places seemed like homes — not without pets. The thought occurred to us that we could slip Sylvester into the house and no one would ever know, but most of the time we play by the rules.

When I asked Toni what she would like for a February anniversary present, she told me that she wanted Sylvester to come home and play with a puppy. I smiled and bought jewelry. When I asked what she wanted for her first-day-of-spring birthday, she told me she wanted Sylvester to come home and play with a puppy. I added to her wardrobe instead. Two strikes.

One morning in May I suggested a mini-vacation over the Memorial Day weekend. When she said she would rather use the money to purchase a puppy, I knew the third strike sizzled toward the plate. That evening, as I drove home from the office, I decided life was too short to allow any of the comparatively few pleasures to slip away. If happiness lurked just a pet away, we would have to risk the wrath of the landlord.

Over dinner, I told Toni I thought she should call her aunt and tell her to pack Sylvester's things. That evening her aunt put a new record in the book. She packed Sylvester's suitcase before the receiver settled in the cradle.

Sylvester's return helped. It also fueled hints, daily hints, that Sylvester needed a puppy. I held firm. Sylvester maintained a low profile and remained a secret from the owner and the neighbors. Adding a puppy would be pushing it.

Then came one of those weak moments that afflict us and eventually shape our destiny. During a session of idle conversation, I happened to say, "If we buy a dog, we should carefully choose the best breed for us and spend the money to buy a good representative of the breed." The logic appealed to Toni. We discussed the handful of breeds we knew and put the idea on hold, I thought.

That afternoon, something compelled me to pluck an issue of *Official Dogs* from the rack of magazines. (That very periodical is lying next to me as I write this paragraph.) A boldface question on the cover caught my eye: "Can We Save Our Endangered Breeds?"

We read the article together while we waited to check out. The thrust was that several breeds showed little, if any, increase in numbers registered, according to the data provided by the A.K.C., and could be facing extinction. Not only did I not recognize the breeds mentioned, but it took me some moments to attribute the initials A.K.C. to the American Kennel Club. Since we intended to buy a purebred dog, Toni reminded me, it would be grand to save a breed from extinction at the same time. I agreed.

The first few breeds we checked out offered little or no aesthetic appeal for either of us. A picture of a Bernese Mountain Dog came next. We both found it hard to believe that dog lovers would allow a breed as beautiful as the Bernese to become extinct. For several pages the Bernese Mountain Dog enjoyed new champions.

Suddenly I heard a gasp. I looked down at the book to see a white bodied dog with a large head and orange ears staring back at me through sad eyes — the Clumber Spaniel.

FINDING OUR CLUMBER

Lest you think the months that passed represented a frivolous abandonment of the cause, I want you to understand that I spent the time reading dog literature and preparing for this very day when I placed the call. I knew what we wanted and did not intend to take no for an answer.

A pleasant voice answered my call. "I want a Clumber," I told her. "A show grade female." (I did not want to use that other word on the phone.) "And I want her in time for my wife's birthday next month."

We often laugh now when people call us with similar requests. "Just wave your wand and produce a show grade bitch for next week." Those callers are often greeted with the same lengthy silence I experienced. But I was on a roll that day and nothing fazed me. Destiny was about to be realized.

"We did just have a litter of nine," the voice answered at length, "seven dogs and two bitches." (Once she used the word the ice was broken.) "We intend to keep one bitch for ourselves. If the other turns out to be show grade, we might be willing to sell her to you. Why don't you come out and meet our Clumbers and we shall discuss it with you."

It meant spoiling the surprise, but I agreed. No hesitation on Toni's part. That weekend we jumped into the car and headed west toward Ohio.

This was not the last of the day's surprises! We thought we were driving eight hours to the other side of Ohio to purchase our puppy and bring her home. We learned upon our arrival that we drove all that way to be interviewed by breeders and Clumbers alike. It soon became obvious that the breeders had no intention of selling a show quality Clumber bitch to just anyone who happened along.

We met adult dogs and listened to the breeders' description of the positive and negative aspects of the breed. They then questioned our intentions and presented a list of equipment and supplies we should purchase to provide for a Clumber's happy existence. We owned none of the things on the list, nor did our facility measure up. We assured our hosts that we would comply to the last detail. Somehow we passed that portion of the test.

They then allowed us to play with the puppies. Abruptly one of the puppies left the pack and toddled over to me. After a long look and several sniffs, the puppy rested its head on my shoe and proceeded to chew my laces. "Looks like that one picked us," Toni said. A stacked deck. The puppy turned out to be the second choice bitch.

Did we go home with the puppy? We did not. Not that day. The breeders promised her to us, but insisted on keeping her another six weeks. They wanted to be certain she was show quality before they released her to us. At the time, we did not know enough to appreciate their caution on our behalf. As it turned out, our choice held together and she came home with us six weeks later. The mouth ultimately went off on their first choice bitch and they sold her as a pet.

OUR FIRST SHOW

Our breeders mentioned showing the animal, but did not elaborate. They certainly did not insist. We agreed, without any clear understanding of what show meant.

We almost missed the whole thing. Under the impression that people only showed adult dogs, we waited until Tina reached two.

"Look! They're having a dog show in Butler. Let's enter Tina." How could I disagree? Fifteen dollars and fifty miles. Toni asked around and somehow got our Clumber entered. What excitement we felt when the official entry arrived in the mail.

Picture us arriving at the show, fifteen minutes ahead of ring time with a bathed, but not groomed, Clumber on the back seat. What did we know? There weren't any guides to showing dogs available in the bookstore, and we knew no one to ask.

Toni trudged up to the ring with her white dog on a black lead. A woman called "Clumber number six." Poor Toni. She had not an idea in the world about gaiting or stacking. Fortunately she had no competition.

Toni and Tina display the affection
both animals and humans need.

And fortunately she encountered a judge with compassion. As if he could not guess, Toni told him it was their first show. With kindness and patience the judge stacked and examined our Clumber, then sent Toni and Tina out and back and around. At the end, we were presented a handful of ribbons. What good fortune. If we had encountered any other of several judges we can think of, our show career could have ended abruptly.

The day did not end there. We asked what all the ribbons meant. The breed judge, who had also scheduled to judge Group, explained we could now compete at the next level. I leave it to the reader to imagine how we strutted around those grounds. First try and we had a blue ribbon, a breed ribbon, and an invitation from the judge to challenge in Group.

Little did we realize that the next step meant a ring full of professional handlers with their trained and groomed dogs – the best of the Sporting breeds with the best of the handlers. Of course Toni had the advantage of not knowing whether the competition was good, bad, or indifferent.

Experienced dog people will have trouble believing this, but it happened. The judge explained to one of the handlers, a breeder of Irish Setters and English Cockers, that it was Toni's first show and asked if she could help her. And that gracious lady did, until Toni took Tina around. Tina almost pulled her mom out of the ring in an effort to reach her dad and give him kisses. There was not much the woman could do to help there.

We went home satisfied that we had successfully discharged our obligation to show. We hung the ribbons above Tina's crate and the three of us retired from the show ring.

BREEDING FOR THE FIRST TIME_____

Again we almost missed it all. As the weeks passed, however, it occurred to me that Toni was so attached to Tina that we should probably breed to ensure we had a second Tina. The contract stated that the breeder reserved the right to choose the first stud. We called. Just point us to the right stud, we said.

Our breeder picked one of the two top Clumbers in the country at that time. The diplomatic voice we spoke with never mentioned spending large dollars campaigning her boy, nor showed any reluctance to breed him to an unseen, non-pointed bitch. She told us to get back to her closer to Tina's season.

Pictures came and we strolled in the clouds again. Virginia Gentleman, owned by Bill and Sandy Blakely, was one of the most handsome dogs ever created, and soon that gorgeous boy would breed with our Tina. We had to be doing something right.

About three weeks before Tina came into season, Virge's owner called and invited us to enter a show in West Virginia, assuring us competition and an opportunity to see Virge in the flesh. In retrospect, it does not take mental gymnastics to calculate that she also wanted to see our bitch before the final commitment of her valuable stud dog.

So, here we go again! We packed in the car a crate, lead, and slicker as our only equipment, with Tina on the back seat, ready to take on some of the best Clumbers in the country. After all, we already had ribbons and had competed in Group.

How those good people, who soon became our friends, must have laughed! They examined Tina, diplomatically praised her, and said good night. The following morning at the show, they beat us readily and finished one of their bitches. Then, and only then, did they take us aside and start teaching us how to groom, gait, stack, and breed. Do you realize just how lucky we were to meet those particular people?!

How important was it to us? Well, Tina won the next morning, the next time out, and the next. We quickly purchased equipment and supplies, and Toni and Tina practiced while I coached.

Virge bred Tina, then Tina finished the show season at Westchester without ever experiencing another defeat. No, she did not just finish. At one of the year's most beautiful and prestigious shows, Tina won her championship in grandeur, beating three previous champions for a five point major. For beginners from Pennsylvania, that was as good as it gets.

Not until three weeks after the last show, during her eighth week of pregnancy, did we learn that the stress of travel and competition caused Tina to resorb her litter of puppies. When the vet had palpated her at four weeks, he smiled and predicted several puppies. But when he examined her just before the due date, the smile disappeared. No puppies; they were gone, dissolved. Five years later, we finally got to enjoy Virge-Tina puppies.

This is a sport of animals and people, not balls and clubs and racquets. We all do well with the exhilaration of victory. Some of us do not do so well in defeat. But in the final analysis, it is only playing. In a world where children still die of starvation and homeless people roam the streets, the majority will hardly note, nor long remember, who goes Best in Show at Westminster.

As we see it, the sport offers a wonderful opportunity to interact with people and animals. Better yet, once the competition ends, there are usually ample opportunities to socialize with those representing a fascinating cross section of humanity and dogdom. Travel as far and often as you desire. If you enjoy sightseeing and/or history, plan to take in the area's offerings before, during, or after the show. Even in defeat, you, Throck, and the rest of the family should have fun.

Warning! Do not, as we did, come to the game unprepared. It most likely will not be your good fortune both to own a superior animal and stumble onto helpful people willing to put breed before vanity.

A second warning! Do not let the sport consume you. Play a game and have fun. When the sport starts to require a disproportionate amount of resources, energy, and emotion step back and take a second look. Have a chat with your new friend. Throck will tell you if it has gone a step too far.

8.

The Foot Wetting

"I talked it over with Throck and the family and we are all excited. Competition, travel, having fun together! Let us get at it. How do we find a show to enter?"

You do not find a show to enter. Not yet.

"But why not? I thought we were ready."

You are ready. Both you and Throck are ready to get ready. Think about it a minute. If any person could buy a purebred then walk into a ring and be competitive, what would that say for the level of competition?

Maybe some people and dogs are naturals but you and Throck do not qualify. You have the right mental attitude and the proper perspective. It is too soon for show yet. First we want you to try a match. A match is a competition, usually limited to puppies and those adults without a major (defeating enough dogs in a match to win more than three points). Although the matches always draw some who go all out, anything for a win, most teams enter for practice, exposure, and fun. You can locate matches through your local kennel clubs. Most clubs make it a point to keep other nearby clubs informed on matches.

There are two types of puppy matches: a fun match and a sanctioned match. At a fun match, almost anything goes. Sometimes they even allow mixed breeds as entrants in the obedience competition. The purpose of a match is to provide an event that simulates a point show, and allows both people and animals the opportunity to practice and have fun without all of the pressures of a show.

A sanctioned match is approved by the A.K.C. It is still meant to be for practice and fun, but it more closely resembles the point show and admits purebreds only.

"Sounds like the perfect start for us. Do we just show up?"

As a rule, you may either pre-enter at a slightly reduced rate, or enter on the morning of the match and pay a little more. The flyer advertising the event normally includes the cut-off dates for mail entries and the closing time for match day entries.

Make sure you take Throck's registration slip. To enter, you will have to give them Throck's official A.K.C. name and number, her birthdate, and the names of her sire and dam. This one time, take nothing else. Give Throck a quick bath, then pack her, the crate, and the family into the wagon and go.

THE FIRST MATCH

"Are these the same judges we'll see at point shows?"

Rarely, if ever. But the judges at matches are usually long-time dog people — breeders, handlers, and the like. They are most often knowledgeable and dedicated dog people. Some aspire to be A.K.C. judges, once they satisfy that organization's requirements.

The other person, or persons, in the ring, identified by the badge worn, is the ring steward. Almost always a member of the sponsoring kennel club, the steward assists the judge by over-seeing the mechanics of the competition in that ring. More on that later.

At a match, the clubs provide everything. They often use ropes, rather then fences, to enclose the rings. Rope is a lot cheaper. As you can see, the rings are not really rings at all, but are squares and rectangles. At most shows the rings branch off to the right and left of a central aisle, much like the pews in a church. The ring number is always mounted on a post, or some other such arrangement, and clearly visible.

The entrance to an individual ring can be found only from the central aisle. At an outdoor point show, where you may find thirty or more rings being utilized, the central aisle is always cov-ered by a giant canopy that extends roughly ten feet into each ring on both sides of the aisle.

Since the sizes of show sites differ, larger and smaller, they sometimes cannot attach all the rings. On those occasions, they situate the overflow on level areas, as close to the dominant rec-tangle as they can find level areas. Then, too, if obedience judging is offered, separate rings are provided and those rings seldom at-tach to the core. The important thing to remember is always to scout the site when you arrive. You will find it more than a little embarrassing to be ready to show and not be able to locate your ring.

You may be wondering why we told you not to bring anything but Throck and a crate. Some of these people have crates, tables, pens, and their own canopies. We told you just to bring Throck because it's her first time out and she needs to have fun, as much as you and your family do. With luck, Throck will put up her tail and follow the lead wherever it goes. Also with luck, you will retain your ability to speak and hear, accompanying your animal around the ring without stepping into a hole, or battering down a post.

You are inexperienced, but practice and fun, that's why the clubs have matches. Keep that in mind when the butterflies start.

As to those others with all the equipment, we can explain some of them. You have those owners who are so competitive that they will throw everything they have into the fray, whether match, point show, or field trial. Their best animal, best equipment, and best effort, always. And there is little to argue with there either, if that's as far as it goes. Unfortunately, out of that group come those who take it a step further, demanding a win at any cost.

Though they might surprise you, many of those very professional looking people represent the perpetual losers at point shows. They talk a good fight, but they won't do the work to perfect their skills. They seldom have top animals. They will spend the money for all the trappings, but only buy marginal dogs. As a consequence, the only place they ever experience any success is at the match level.

"Not all those animals look like puppies."

They're not all puppies. You and Throck are competing at the six to nine month Senior level. There are also nine to twelve month Seniors, along with two to four and four to six month old Juniors. Any animal over twelve months is considered an adult. A few of those have competed in point shows and have even won points. Major winners are banned, but not single point winners.

Why would someone with a pointed animal bother with a match? For practice and fun. Sometimes the animal is laid back and needs to build up its confidence under relaxed conditions.

Yes, you will also find the person who brings their well adjusted adult. They fit with the all out group we mentioned earlier. Win, even if it means bringing an adult with a major and lying about it.

"And if they don't win?"

Pardon our smile. That does happen, especially at matches, where there is little pressure on the judges to be political. The big fish does not always dominate the small pond.

"That is a beautiful puppy over there — the Shepherd. Those people appear very professional and do not look at all like perpetual losers."

You have a good eye. Losers? Hardly! Big time winners. The woman brushing the animal is the professional handler the owners use on their dogs. What they probably have with them is a puppy for which they have great expectations. They want it to get off to a resounding debut. The start of a long campaign toward national, even international, prominence in the breed. Notice the extra crates. Those are the parents. The quality puppy increases the parents' value for those interested in breeding to the bitch, or using the male at stud. The parents proved they can apparently pass some nice things to their progeny.

All is not lost though, not at all. Strange things happen at dog shows. Throck is a better Clumber than the other puppy is a Shepherd. All you have to do is make the judge believe that.

IN THE RING

"Clumber Spaniels. Puppy bitch, six to nine months."

The steward is now calling you into the ring. You and Throck are on. You've been watching these other people. Two magic minutes! That's all you have to worry about. You'll have the judge's undivided attention for two magic minutes. Stack, gait, stack, gait. Nothing to it.

An interesting first outing for Throck. She kept her attention on Lynnedora, her tail wagging, all the while she wound the lead around Lynnedora's leg. Cute! And Throck also looked cute rolling on her back while the judge examined her. (She really caught the crowd's attention when she relieved herself in the judge's hand.)

"All right, you found us. We're embarrassed."

Embarrassed? You and the family? No, not all of the family. Throck appears to be her same feisty little self.

Before we discuss any more competition, let's discuss your embarrassment. Much ado about nothing. Your puppy acted like a puppy at a puppy match. That behavior at a point show, where it is assumed the puppy has had some exposure and at least fundamental preparation, can cause red cheeks. But it happens there too. Often! If puppies can, they will, when you least expect it. Now maybe you understand why we discouraged your plan to charge off to a point show without practice. So much for the family's embarrassment. As to the competition, Throck, with all her foul deeds, won for her breed. She had no competition, but that doesn't mean she had no value. Now Throck must represent her breed against all other six to nine month breed winners from the Sporting group. If she triumphs there, she must then go against the six to nine month winners of the other six groups. That's when she'll go up against the Shepherd for best six to nine month puppy in match.

At some matches, two to four month and four to six month are considered Junior puppies. They compete against each other and one Junior puppy victor emerges to contend for match. The same applies to Seniors, six to nine and nine to twelve. Many times there is an additional competition, including the Best Junior and Senior puppies along with the Best Adult, for best overall animal in match.

What would the reader guess from the team of Throck and Lynnedora? Throck could rally and go Best. Or, she could get dumped in Group. If Throck makes it out of Group, there is that Shepherd puppy to contend with, handled by a professional to make things worse.

After learning from this experience at a match, let's begin to prepare seriously for a point show.

9.

Training the Handler

"After yesterday's fiasco, we'll try whatever you suggest."

CONDITIONING

First we shall do some running then. If you get tired, we'll walk; then run again. For this training just use the six foot lead. Throck needs to understand she's working and it's all business. The retractable lead should be used for family outings only.

Run at a nice, easy pace. Cover as many different surfaces as possible: macadam, grass, concrete, sand, gravel, flat, uphill, downhill, uneven. Do your shoes support well and have a versatile tread? You never know what surface you might encounter at a show. Even veterans get fooled when a club changes the site of their annual show, or shows. The animals often respond badly to new surfaces. It's amazing how those brought up on concrete and stone distort their gait and break concentration on grass.

Another reason we want to run, Lynnedora, is to assure ourselves that you are toning and conditioning along with Throck. And we have solid reasons for wanting that. The fact that you're only in the ring two minutes is misleading! That's your time alone with the judge. What about the grooming, packing, driving, unpacking, and exercising? The rest of the time you are in the ring and under stress. Saturday ends and Sunday we repeat it all. Sleeping in a strange bed, eating irregular meals, and dealing with rain, mud, cold, or heat requires conditioning! That's what keeps you going. Conditioning!

Sport and recreation happily enjoyed, that's the whole idea here. We do not want this endeavor to become a Bataan death march because you're exhausted. Certainly you do not want to see Throck collapsing on a hot day for want of conditioning.

In a few minutes we will walk for a bit. When you start exhibiting at the point shows, sooner or later you will hear the top judges describe a good handler as one who just seems to fade into the background so that all the judge sees is the animal. This is an ideal situation, of course, because a judge is supposed to evaluate only the animal. Though built around an important element of truth, in large part it is a myth, or at least wishful thinking. Imagine yourself as the judge and your assignment is Sporting dogs.

The rules say the animal must be accompanied by and under the control of a handler. A beautiful Clumber Spaniel bitch circles the ring. The judge stands too far away to be sure whether he knows the handler. In fact, his eyes remain on the smoothly moving animal with the perfect Clumber roll. If the handler does nothing to help the animal, he also does nothing to detract. The judge likes the animal.

Consider the competition! Look at the handler. No jacket or tie, towel jammed into his back pocket and with its swinging distracting his animal, the other animals, and the judge. The handler sweats like a horse under saddle, you can hear him pant from across the ring. The animal would move a lot smoother if the handler could keep up. She might even be the best animal, but we shall never know with Claude the clod handling. There is nothing but a pile of flab, too tired to bend down and stack the poor bitch. Claude does not leave the judge any choice.

Before leaving the subject of the unobtrusive handler, let's talk a little more about clothing. Shoes must be trustworthy and comfortable — as well as the rest of the wardrobe for that matter — but certainly the shoes. Women would do well to complete their ring wardrobe with separates that allow bending and movement. Men? The tried and true slacks, jacket, and tie work best.

In addition to considering your wardrobe in terms of yourself, think also of how your choices relate to Throck. Needless to say, you should avoid outfits so dramatic they steal the scene, or so flowing they distract the star when she gaits.

You will provide the background for the photo that the little camera in the judge's eye takes. Are you showing early morning, late afternoon, or midday? Is it overcast or bright? Keep the background simple. Remember, sometimes subtle differences in tone provide a better background than contrasting colors. When the judge's little camera snaps, make sure it records the best picture you can provide.

Your breathing's back to normal. Time to run again.

WHY A ROUTINE IS NEEDED_____

Now is the time to develop a routine, Lynnedora. Whatever other jobs you might take on — driver, groomer, secretary — your responsibilities as handler begin the minute you hear the steward's voice call you into the ring. Your support crew can do everything for you and Throck up to that point, if you wish; but once the voice calls, you and Throck go it alone.

When you go to your first show, allot as much time as possible to watching the professional handlers at work. They make it look easy. But do not be deceived. Much planning and practice went into that finished product.

You will also notice the handler's versatility. See him now with a Toy Poodle and ten minutes later with a Bullmastiff. When one considers the fact that these handlers usually meet the dog less than a week before showing it, their consistency, handler to animal and one to another, appears the more amazing.

Please do not mistake us. We would be the last to say that all professional handlers — those who charge for their handling services and/or belong to the Professional Handlers Association — are equally competent, or even competent at all. Remember, the proficient handler, regardless of the breed being handled, makes it look easy.

Making it look easy is not an accident. As we mentioned earlier, much planning and practice lead to a routine, which in turn provides consistency. Following are some specifics to watch for.

When the steward calls, the pros and their animals start showing immediately, before they enter the ring. But the inexperienced handler is likely to plod into the ring, the attention of his animal anywhere but on the handler. If the judge looks at the contestants prior to the official start of the competition, he sees one team poised and ready, the other at ease or only in the process of getting ready. Which team do you think starts with an advantage? From start to finish, the professional handler appears to be one step ahead of the competition.

The proficient professional will always be one of the best in the ring, but that is not to say that there are not owner handlers

— non-professionals — who can at least match them, step-for-step, on any given day. They can and do, often.

But many more owner-handlers lose to the professionals, with regularity. The difference? As with the pros, those who develop a routine, a system, win. With a system, the handler programs himself to respond to the expected without thinking. That way his mind is then free to contend with the unexpected.

While you are studying, give some time to the poor handlers also. Notice how many times an excellent animal is compromised by the inadequacy of his escort.

"Should we consider hiring a handler until I'm ready?"

An answer to that question requires another look at why you entered the sport. If the only objective is to own a champion, hire a handler. If your motive is animal and family, working together toward a common goal, a professional handler defeats the purpose.

"We hoped you would say that. We were feeling a little guilty about holding her back. Do we start with Throck or me?"

We start and end with the handler. The animals train easily.

If you learn nothing else, go away with these words in mind. A system breeds consistency. We want to prepare your head before we train your body. No single thing that a handler does presents any extreme degree of difficulty. The difficulties arise when the inexperienced handlers allow the package to overwhelm them. Let's first take a look at what it is that confronts you, what needs are to be mastered, and then we shall discuss a way through it all.

10.

Training Your Puppy

SOCIALIZING YOUR DOG

First, Lynnedora, we want to concentrate on socializing and toning Throck. Take her as many places and as often as you can. Walk her on the main street of town, in small parking lots, any place where you find people, other dogs, noise. Children want to pet her? Adults? Encourage them.

Make every outing a positive outing, for you, for Throck, and for the strangers. Taking a small pooper scooper, paper towels, and a plastic bag for accidents will ensure that you are welcome to return. On the way home, buy Throck a treat. We always did well with vanilla shakes, or vanilla ice cream in a dish without a spoon. Next trip, Throck will be at the door waiting.

What the occasional milkshake puts on, the mile run each day will take right off. (Larger dogs may need a longer run to keep toned; Toys a whole lot less.) Run your fingers over those ribs to make sure no fat pads are there. Since Throck will soon work harder, you may want to give her slightly more food, say a quarter cup, and slightly more protein per helping.

OBEDIENCE CLASSES

"The kennel club sponsors an obedience class. Can Throck do both at the same time?"

Screams from the left and screams from the right and here we stand in the middle. This is a long-time controversy, as we mentioned in Chapter Four. One very vocal faction of the dog world insists that putting a show dog in obedience training breaks that very spirit so important to the big winners. Closely akin are those who insist that the obedience dog will sit in the show ring. Just as vocal are those who laugh at such notions and maintain that obedience training improves the bond, thus the show dog.

With all due caution, we shall stand with the minority and advise you to go the class. Treat it as additional socialization for Throck — people, dogs, and noise.

What happens after that depends in large part upon the character of both dog and human and should be closely monitored. Make certain that Throck wears a different style collar and lead than that she wears for conformation. Never mix the two; again, consistency is very important.

The sit is an important response in obedience. So is stand. If she can learn one, she can learn the other. At those times when you think she might sit during the routine, reinforce her with a stand command.

As to spirit, we believe the handler dictates there. If the handler corrects harshly and punishes indiscretions, then a loss of spirit is more than possible. If, however, the handler approaches obedience training positively, as a chance for both handler and animal to share quality time, the teamwork that evolves can only benefit both.

Throck is on the road to toning and socialization. It is time to get serious about the grooming, especially those of you who were masochistic enough to purchase Poodles, Terriers, Komondorok, Shi Tzus, and the like. After you see the work facing those people, Lynnedora, you will love your Clumber all the more. Just think, some of the brush-and-show breeds have it easier yet.

GROOMING

"How important is the grooming?"

The answer to that question will vary with the breed and the judge. In the minds of the many dog people, officials and participants, the conformation ring is where beauty contests are held. To underscore that position, the French still refer to their conformation champions as Champions de Beauté.

If not a beauty contest, then what? Of late, we have noticed a decided change in emphasis among many of the judges. Once a Clumber had to sparkle in the sun to be in contention. Now people compete grass stained animals and win. We even remember when coat quality and texture impressed judges. The animal with blown coat — that summer molt of the undercoat — suffers no disadvantages in many of today's rings, even though the coat lacks quality.

Why the change of emphasis? We shall save our theories on that subject for the section on judging. Suffice it to say here that many judges are extremely concerned as to what animals appear in the group ring out of the breeds they judge. Since the Group area (discussed at length in Volume II) emphasizes movement, the breed judges often times only concern themselves with that aspect of the animal. (More on this later.)

Lynnedora can neglect grooming and stacking practice to perfect gaiting technique. The minute she does, she will draw a beauty contest judge. Of course she could reverse that. Groom every hair individually, stack faultlessly, and walk out of the ring knowing she wasted her efforts on a movement judge.

As we see it, there are two ways to avoid such incidents. Many keep a notebook on judges. After they show to that person, they jot reminders as to their tendencies — head hunter, movement judge, political, etc. The judges are advertised in advance in the *Gazette*. Check your breeder and kennel club friends for insight. No one fools all the people for very long. After you have been in the sport a while, you will fill your own notebook.

The other possibility, and by far the safest, is to give grooming, stacking, and gaiting equal consideration as you prepare. Go into the ring every time knowing both you and Throck are as prepared as you are capable of being.

What do you do if you have no information or no one close who shows the same breed? Start by reading your standard. Often times the standard describes or limits grooming. Call your breeder and ask for any pictures or pointers that might help. There are several grooming books available. Many professional groomers have books that picture show-coats. For a fee (time is money), they may be willing to discuss technique and equipment. (Be careful. Certain pet groomers would not recognize a show cut if it grew teeth and bit them.)

We really wish we could be of more help, but there are just too many breeds, with too many separate grooming requirements, to even attempt a description. Please seek out a breed owner or professional if you own one of the complicated breeds

— Terrier, Poodle, Miniature Schnauzer, Bichon, Shih Tzu, Maltese, Lhasa, Cocker.

With some of the other, easier breeds, when all else fails, tidy her feet and ears and go to the show. Go the night before if possible. Very early the day of the show, seek out anyone present with your breed. Will they help? Clumber people most likely would, if for no other reason than their aversion to having the public see a poorly groomed specimen of their breed.

STACKING

Socialized, toned, and groomed, it is time to learn posing, or stacking. Posing and stacking are interchangeable, with stacking by far the more common. Popularity aside, posing is probably a more accurate suggestion. We discussed with you the theory of developing a routine. Now we'll step out of theory and into reality.

Before you touch Throck, let's decide together what you hope to accomplish and why. Understand that the stacking phases are in keeping with the beauty contest concept. Think of Miss America; they groom her, stack her, move her. But Miss America gets an advantage. They allow her to demonstrate her talent, but Throck does not get a chance to show the conformation judge how she flushes birds and retrieves, her real talent.

We shall assume you draw a superior judge, one who is able and willing to judge the whole dog. More, she both knows and understands the standard and as a final bonus, she is non-political, to the extent that's possible.

The judge moves to her first position. (It could as easily be a male. There are certainly men of equal quality.) What is she doing?

She is studying photos of posed animals, assessing overall outline, evaluating impression in terms of type. Your job, then, is to provide a well-composed photo for her. By the time she moves out, it's too late to change anything. All your work must be completed in those few seconds after you enter, and before she takes her position.

Because she will have a better dimensional perspective of those animals near the center of the line, be there if you can. Sometimes the judge requests catalog order and leaves you no choice. Remember that a straight-on focus sees only two legs. Get

Throck on a slight angle to the judge, and play the light, depending on whether it is early, overcast, or bright. Balance Throck between the animals to the right and to the left and make sure the ground is level.

"What if it isn't?"

The easiest way is to excuse yourself to the end of the line. Do not hesitate and lose time over false starts. Decide and go. You can also maintain the same position, but drop back a foot or two farther from the judge than the others. Sometimes doing so gains you the added advantage of drawing the judge's focus.

There are only a few basic stacks. The Shepherds use an exaggerated pose to suggest alertness, Springers have rear feet slightly behind square, and Clumbers are four square. Do as the others do. Your object is to pose the most complimentary picture of the animal that you can, in keeping with breed custom or requirements of breed standard.

When stacking a dog we start by setting the head, then the front feet, rear feet, tail, and head once more. Again, we cannot verbally stack every breed, so we shall help Lynnedora with Throck, and the reader can modify where necessary. You will find that with most breeds the principles are much the same.

Because the Clumber is a head breed, we like the collar right in the notch at the rear of the jaw and up behind the ears. A slight push forward puffs that loose skin around the head and makes the head look even larger. From that position, just a little upward tension on the collar will cause the dog to react by arching his neck to counter the tension.

Four square simply means four feet providing a square foundation under the animal. Set the left front leg first by rolling her weight to her right front, reaching over or under, whichever suits you. Grasping the leg at the elbow, place the paw under the shoulder, not in front or in back of it. Roll her weight to that side to hold the left foot in place and move the right leg. Equalize the weight over both feet.

Move your attention to the left rear. Again, use the elbow.

"Won't she move the front in the meantime?"

That is certainly a possibility. With a young animal, we could upgrade that to probability. Now you know that one reason we start with the head and hook a finger under the collar to hold it up is that a dog usually wants to lower his head to get his feet moving. We also pull his chest slightly forward, throwing his center of gravity onto those forelegs.

Front and rear feet too far forward.
Topline roached

Rear feet too far back.
Topline swayed

"And the feet never move?"

How wonderful that would be if the feet never moved. They move, but after some training, they do not move often, and usually only one foot does. Fix what is broken and nothing more.

Make sure the rear ankles — hocks in dog show language — stand perpendicular to the ground and face directly to front and rear. When you look down a line from the rump to the ground, you should see the rear of the hock as part of the line. Check that top line to make sure it is straight and firm. Now you have achieved four square: back straight with the ground, legs with legs.

When you think you have it right, take two or three photographs from slightly different positions. Now examine the results. Look for weaknesses in the stack ahead of time, so that you can avoid mistakes in the ring. Dog's head is down and forward; already the animal is out of balance. Front feet are forward, the top line sags; rear feet forward, a roached (arched) back results; rear feet too far back, a sway back appears.

Practice! Always do it the same way. The objective is a perfect stack on the first try, without excessive movement.

The judge has her first photo. If she liked Throck best, Throck starts out the winner and the rest have to beat her if they can.

Take them around, the judge signals. (We shall deal with that subject under gaiting.) What we want to warn you against here is falling asleep when you come back in. Do not dally; get Throck stacked again immediately.

A four square stack

We know most of the other handlers are trying to relax themselves and their dogs. The judge closes in to face the line head on and start her inspections. She goes to the first bitch and that gives your fourth position bitch some time. But each time the judge moves, she also glances down the line and compares what she has just seen. How do you want her to see Throck? Relaxed and daydreaming, or alert and ready?

Do not desert your animal during the inspection. She needs to feel you nearby while strange hands probe and squeeze. When the judge examines the head, touch Throck's back to reassure her and check the foot positions. If the feet move, realign them immediately.

When the judge moves, the handler moves. Let Throck see you. Bait her, with a piece of liver perhaps, if you prefer, or hold her muzzle in your hand if you do not bait.

Do not let Throck relax once the judge is finished, especially if the judge did comment on her splendid rear. If she thought enough of that rear to comment, let her see it as often as you can. You always need to keep yourself and Throck alert. Obviously it would hurt your chances greatly if the judge also likes the rear on the sixth dog, but when she glances back to Throck to compare the two she finds her sitting!

The judge will send each animal out in a pattern and take a concentrated look at each dog. Keep Throck stacked until you pattern, then stack her again as soon as you return. If you have not blown that early advantage, you are still the one to beat.

Do not allow your attention to wander. Keep one eye on Throck and the other on the judge. She may well glance over to compare every other animal that patterns with Throck. (Many judges, pattern each dog immediately after its examination.)

Smooth the hair on the animal's rear as a reminder. If you believe Throck also has a better neck and head than the competition, show the judge. Push that collar forward and stroke that neck. Maybe she studied the movement so intently she missed Throck's superiority of head and neck.

If, after patterning the animals, the judge returns to center ring, chances are she has her winner and is shopping for second through fourth. Of course it could also mean that she found two of the animals very even and intends to give the win to the bitch who gives her that final best impression. Hold that stack.

If, however, she walks the line for her last look, odds are the decision involves fronts and rears. It could well be that Throck is her winner and she needs second through fourth, or maybe Throck and the sixth position bitch remain very close in her mind. She needs an additional strength or weakness to tip the balance, so show her that head and lovely length of neck. The other bitch's head sets on her shoulders.

The judge pulls the dogs out and rearranges the order for a last look. The signal comes to take them around.

GAITING

With that signal, we shall shift our focus to movement, or gaiting. Many dog people use those terms interchangeably. It is common to hear one person talk about moving his dog and another talking about gaiting his dog.

We prefer the term gaiting, because it refines mere movement and suggests an animal covering the ground in a comfortable and efficient manner. What is more, the handler talks about moving his dog, whereas gaiting implies the dog does its best thing and the handler only accompanies him around.

Movement connotes to us that the handler assists his animal in transferring his presence from one place to another. Under this definition almost anyone could move an animal. Push, tug, string it — move that dog.

*The handler should have let the dog
lead off to set her own gait.*

Technically, both terms are inadequate. When we think of the dog in motion, we must also give thought to the intended function of the dog. The excellent animal displays a proportionate relationship of ligament to tendon, to muscle, and to bone, which allows the animal coordinated movement as he performs the function for which he was bred.

We hasten to add that very few judges appear to consider function. To assess whether a dog covers the ground with a minimum of effort is hard work, especially for the judge who would also evaluate coordination and balance. It is easier to look for the animal with a smooth side gait and head held high. It is easier to ignore the fact that a dog can exhibit good side gait while it crabs or paddles around the ring, and to disregard the fact that forward motion requires the head to drop and the body and neck to extend.

Handlers probably hurt their animals' chances for victory more during the motion sequences than at any other time. They race, bounce, flail, drag, anything to throw their animal off its natural stride. The judge may suspect the dog is capable of better things, but she should only judge what she sees that day.

Baiting

Bait hurts as many handlers as it helps. Liver, hot dog, banana, cheese, squeaky toy, all of these equal bait. Almost anything carried by a handler, or an associate outside the ring, intended to win his charge's attention and, hopefully, bolster the animal's enthusiasm, may be considered bait.

We can understand why a handler might need bait to get the attention of a dog with whom he has had little contact. More difficult though, is the understanding of an owner-handler who needs it. Beyond understanding is why those who come after should have to wade through the bait from a previous competition.

What if the A.K.C. implemented a rule to make a judge, personally or through stewards, responsible for retrieving bait after each competition? Do you suppose judges might start penalizing abusers? Bait might even disappear in time; the world liver market possibly collapsing.

Taking the Dog around the Ring

The signal is given to take them around. (Several judges send the dogs around first and then evaluate outline. The preliminary jaunt is theorized to relax handlers and settle animals.) More parts of the whole to consider, Lynnedora. How do you move gracefully from stack position to gaiting position? What is the correct way for you to gather in excess lead? Can you now let the lead out and take it in on the run? All of these questions are parts of the whole of showing.

Your job is simple. Become invisible! Once you accomplish that, keep up with Throck.

A handler wants to allow the dog to perform without liability or distraction. It would be great to unhook the lead and let the dog circle the ring naturally. But the rules do not allow that. Rehook the lead and get ready.

Professional handlers do a lot of little things in the ring. Some are necessary; others justify their reason for being to a gullible audience. What would happen if they became invisible? Who would hire them to disappear?

That does not mean every novice should do the same. Instead, concentrate on these few suggestions. As you prepare to start, run the collar to the jaw notch and tense the lead to get Throck's attention. Now she knows it is all business, not play. A lot of people combine that with a love tap to the dog's chin or rump. Lead off with your left foot, especially if you train for obedience also. Walk, do not run. At the same time, your left hand should advance the lead, directing Throck to start. The moment she does, relax the lead tension.

Walk until Throck breaks into her gait, then adjust your pace to hers, keeping the lead slack, even flapping. A lead is intended to restrain an animal intent on deviant behavior, not to act as sail and rudder.

Permit no distractions such as swinging towels or dropped combs and brushes. Avoid skirts that swing to and fro and flapping sportcoats. The right arm of a human is not a wing intended to flail the air. Long strides that conclude with the whole foot hitting the ground at the same time are a distraction. You should appear as two coordinated and toned athletes covering ground side-by-side.

Unfortunately, problems arise when the unexpected takes place. For instance, after you enter the ring, an unexpected rain shower occurs. The ground is slippery! There is no way to switch footwear. Give Throck as much lead as you can if you run into traction problems. Be especially careful not to go down on the turns.

"The man in the first position just took off without us!"

That happens. Most often, the handler in the first position pays the other handlers the courtesy of checking with them to see if everyone is ready before he starts dashing off.

If you were in second position and the first handler unexpectedly took off on you, instinctively you might try to catch him. That would be a mistake. He gaits his bitch properly, but you and Throck must dash to catch up. Who looks better to the judge?

Another quiz to solve. You are in the fourth position and naturally Throck would rather lead than follow. What you should do is let first through third get a three or four step headstart before starting. As soon as a gap appears, start Throck. She leads five through eight and everybody's happy.

But what if the third animal is a poor mover and slow enough to break Throck's natural gait?

"We go out around her."

Why not in around her? Remember the judge is watching and evaluating. Why should you surrender the judge's attention during the pass? There are no rules governing which side you can pass on, so you can choose the inside even — and all the better — if in doing so you obstruct the judge's view of the dog on the outside.

You are coming in from your first circuit now and it is raining harder. As soon as you come in, stack. No matter how wet and uncomfortable, stack!

Now, what did the judge look for as Throck went around? If you did not distract her, she looked for balance, i.e., firm back, rear legs supplying propulsion, front legs reaching and lifting, the feet dropping in time with each other. She saw all those things in Throck, but being the wise, experienced judge that she is, she knows correct movement cannot be awarded on the basis of side movement only.

This gait is natural and the dog cannot be taught to improve its gait. The best you can do is to allow her to move naturally and do not interfere by jerking the lead.

Patterns

The judge inspects and calls each animal out for patterns. No time for nonchalance! Gait Throck out there and keep her ready. Get close enough to the judge to hear her instructions clearly. Out of the fourth position, you watched three others complete the pattern before you. This judge asks handlers to take the animal out to a corner on the diagonal and return. Listen to the judge and be sure to do what she tells you.

Skip all the circling, lead winding, and baiting, the judge wants to see the animal's rear in action. Take Throck out on a straight line in a natural gait. Don't hurry and don't let Throck weave. The judge wants to see the rear.

Coming back. Keeping Throck on your left, turn her as you turn yourself. Avoid jerking or breaking the animal's gait and start back. Do not take any wide turns that have Throck on the angle until she is almost in, and no fancy hand and lead changes. The woman wants to see Throck's front now, so stop a good three feet in front of the judge and come around to a one o'clock position. Talk to Throck and praise her.

The judge will watch the animal for expression as she reacts to you. Some judges jingle keys, whistle, or in some way try to win Throck's attention to themselves. Do not fight them.

Avoid getting in too close before you stop so that you run over the judge. Nor does it help to come in, smile, and quit. Keep working with Throck. Be aware of where the judge is and let her see the dog's expression. Work until she dismisses the two of you.

"How many patterns are there?"

We have only ever seen four requested, three of those often. Out and back you just experienced, with emphasis on front and rear. Perhaps the most common goes out and takes a right angle to the handler's left. The handler then comes in on the diagonal to complete the right triangle.

In a variation, the handler forgoes the diagonal and returns along the same right angled pattern he went out on. If you think about that pattern, what you are doing is an upside down and reversed "L". A variation you seldom hear called anymore requires you to transform that "L" to a "T". You must first complete the original upside down and backward "L", but as you return, and before you make the turn onto the leg that leads you back to the judge, you must go on past the intersection of the two legs, as if you were tracing out a big "T" with your feet. Return to the intersection and come in on the stem of the "T".

The "T" requires some extra practice, because the animal always should be closer to the judge, giving the judge an unobstructed view. Try it once and you will find that several changes of lead from right hand to left, and left to right, are necessary. Smooth transitions allow Throck to perform at her best. Fortunately, the "T" is seldom requested anymore.

It should be obvious that with the last three patterns, the judge adds side gaiting. Why, we do not quite understand. She wanted another look at the top line, perhaps. The distance does seem short to help evaluate side gait. Ours is not to reason why. No matter the pattern, the judge will send you and Throck around after checking expression, so that she can evaluate Throck's side gait without the influence of other dogs, and to see if Throck's topline remains firm. Also, Throck may be tiring. If she is prone to pace (move both feet on the same side at the same time), it could

Show Ring Movement

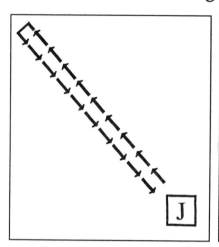

"Out and back" pattern.

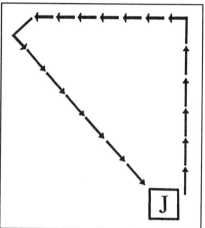

"Triangle" pattern.

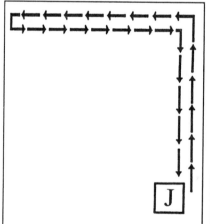

"L" pattern.

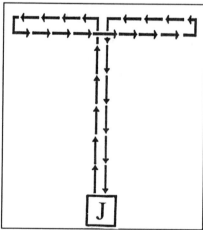

"T" pattern.

show up now.

"What did she look for when I took Throck out and back?"

On the way out, she watched for the paws to fall on a line without crossing over. (Animals can track a double, parallel line also.) She also wanted to see if Throck crabbed. When an animal overreaches with her rear feet and has to throw them sideways to avoid her front feet, she crabs. She also looked for cow hocks. Cow hocks are hocks that turn towards each other as the feet turn outward. Very often the animals with superior reach show a loose and under-powered rear.

Coming in, the judge again checks the way the paws fall on a line. She is also alert for paddling. This mannerism occurs when the dog has trouble getting her front feet out of the way of the rear feet. The animal moves forward on ankles that swing out, but the patterns provide no lift.

As an overdone front can affect a rear, the reverse can also be true. A dog with a tight, propelling rear can also show a tight and restricted front. The great dog may not possess either a perfect front or perfect rear; rather, both may be less than perfect. The balanced movement that results, however, may be perfectly exciting.

The judge positions herself for one last look at the entire class. She sends the six position bitch out and back again for fronts and rears then she points at Lynnedora. Throck is easily just as good as her competition in front and rear and she uses both better. That top line never flutters.

Walk until she gaits, and then join her, straight and true. Allowing her to weave makes it look as though she has trouble tracking. Bring her in straight and true again. You have nothing to hide, so you do not have to hurry her or run an erratic pattern.

Slow and stop. Does the judge want expression? No? Good, give her outline and emphasize that neck and head.

"I'm afraid I am confused. And I don't know why. I understand what I have to do in theory. And I thought I was all set to do it. Just break down the stacking and gaiting to parts. It seemed perfectly clear when we were discussing each step. Now so many things seem lost in a gentle fog. Like that final out and back. You hinted that a handler might purposely zig-zag his dog, or hurry him. Why?"

If the front or back is weak, you don't want the judge to linger over it. Get the animal out fast. The dog changing directions does not give a good view of the rear. Let the dog get ahead and the handler can also interfere with the judge's view.

The judge probably knows what is being done, but she could also think it is an inexperienced handler, or a frisky dog distracted by the scents of those who went before. It is better the judge think that, than to see cow hocks or close movement.

A handler with an animal whose front is east to west, not straight, circles the dog when he stops it for its expression check. Stops it and keeps it moving. Both judge and handler know the dog naturally stacks with front feet going in two different directions, but there is nothing to be gained by drawing attention to it. A lot of that can be hidden with a formal stack.

Once you apply yourself, you will undoubtedly remember more than you think. We put all of the stacking and gaiting sequences together so that each sequence could reinforce the previous. Perhaps if we reviewed with you each one as they actually occur, some of the fog will give way to light.

APPROACHES TO HANDLING

There are many approaches to handling — good, bad, and indifferent. The operative word here is system. If the approach leads you to a system as its final product, one that you can embrace and utilize, then it's perfect for you. If you cannot realize a system from your efforts, the approach is a waste of your time.

Remember our school years, when teachers used to admonish us to reduce fractions? In one sense, reducing fractions is the essence of our approach. Break the whole routine into parts, the parts into smaller parts, and smaller, and so on.

For example, let's look at the part where we adjust the rear feet during a stack. Do you reach over or under, outside or inside, use your left hand or right? Where does the hand grab?

Once you have all the parts reduced, work out the easiest and most efficient way of completing that part. Have the family watch and offer suggestions, criticizing what looks awkward. If you own a camcorder, ask one of the family members to film you. Watch the film carefully and criticize yourself. The search for a better, smoother method never ends.

Most newcomers attempt to emulate the flashy professionals and owner-handlers. They never notice all of the small things that produce the overall affect such as a flourish, a position in relation to the animals, or a whip of the lead on the curves. These are all end products; copies without any understanding of how and why.

What the would-be handler must understand is that none of those end products they see displayed by successful handlers are divine or even correct. A foot position or a baiting stance are acceptable, common, and not wrong. But unless you understand how and why the person arrived at that position, unless you can fit it into your system and make it contribute, it is not right either, and certainly not divine.

Once you feel you have mastered every part you intend to keep, begin the task of arranging the parts into a larger fraction. Sense provides the yardstick to apply to each part. To stack an animal by adjusting rear feet, then head, then front feet makes no sense. When you satisfy yourself that there isn't any better way available and that no sequence makes any more sense, practice until you can run the sequence under any condition without devoting any great amount of thought. Create larger fractions, always larger fractions until you have the whole.

Rehearse a mental run through as soon as you awaken and just before you sleep. Practice by yourself, and practice with Throck, but practice.

A REVIEW

The steward calls for Clumber puppy bitches numbers six, eight, ten, twelve, fourteen, sixteen, eighteen, and twenty. (When you see that many Clumber puppy bitches in a ring at the same time, call us so that we can share it with you.) Enter the ring and stack your animal where the steward directs you. Sequence one.

The judge centers herself a few feet away and evaluates the outline of the animal for type and balance. She then signals us to take them around. Sequence two.

Once you complete your circuit, stack again. Whether a formal stack, in which the handler arranges the animal, or a natural stack, in which the animal is allowed to assume a well-balanced pose on its own, depends on what the judge does next. Some judges examine all of the larger dogs first, then call them out to pattern. Others examine them in place, sending them out and back after each exam. Most often (always with the small animals that are examined on the table), the judge calls each animal out separately, examines, and patterns. Keep in mind your animal should always look good when the judge seeks her out. For that matter, Throck should look good whenever the judge sees her — purposely, accidentally, or otherwise — because you never know when the judge is making a comparison.

"The patterns I understand, I think. It's after that I start having trouble. Expression, for instance. Is that the word you used?"

We hope we used it, because that's the right word. It describes a quality in the dog that newcomers usually overlook; a quality that many judges consider important.

Although some judges look for it during the exam, most wait until after you come in from the pattern. It is exactly here that many amateurs blow it to the pros. The judge wants you to stop your animal and present her for inspection again. This time the judge wants to evaluate expression and check the outline of the naturally posed dog.

The latter presents no challenge. The natural pose is that which the animal assumes without any hands-on adjustments from the handler. The handler may well coax another step or two or urge the head up with collar or bait. Still, for the most part, the pose is one Throck assumes naturally.

If the judge sees expression — which is completely subjective — and likes it, it is a plus for Throck. If there is no expression, no plus and possibly a minus. At least give the judge an opportunity to find it if it's there.

There is one last look while the judge totals pluses and minuses. She may already have her winners and so use that last appraisal only as a confirmation. If any of the positions are still in question, she may walk the whole line, looking for an expression here, a front there, or an out-and-back. She may well ask you to assume a new position in the line. Listen! If she wants you first, do not let a pro con you into the second position.

When she signals for the final circuit, ninety-nine percent of the time the contest is over. Something about the last move could change her mind. Seldom, but it happens.

Once you believe you have a complete routine, practice it a hundred times, with and without Throck. Then call your kennel club and ask when their handling class meets. Most club-sponsored weekly handling classes are too crowded, too informal, and too under-taught, but you don't care. You already have a hard fought routine that works wonderfully well for you and Throck in the serenity of your side yard.

Your objective in attending the class is to test your routine against chaos, to test your flexibility when confronted by spontaneous situations.

When you get home, break out the troublesome sequences and reduce them again. Fix only the broken part. Go back the following week and test your repair, and again the next week until you can promise yourselves consistency.

Now the big test arrives. Don the clothes you intend to show in and give the family a flawless preview. Ask them to criticize anything they do not like. No grades are given – only pass or fail. Either you are now ready for the ring, or you are ready to review the whole routine again. You will know which.

There is also another matter to consider. We only took you as far as the losers go in breed. If Throck occupies that first position when the judge awards ribbons, you two have more work ahead with less room for error.

It is never better for Throck if you hire a professional handler. Professional handlers are a must for the owner who doesn't have time to groom and show, or who is physically or geographically unable to show. Certainly Throck's chances of winning increase with an accomplished pro for a number of reasons. But do not believe the myth the pros perpetuate that no one but a pro can win in certain breeds. A pro may well take Throck to victory sooner and win bigger. But the pro will never give Throck the love and attention and sense of security in the pack that you will.

11.

Pre-show Preparations

CHOOSING A SHOW_____

We hope by this time that you subscribe to one of the dog magazines that offer a calendar of events. Open it and read the announcements of events that will take place a month or more after the present date.

You need to give yourself this much time because entries close three weeks before the show. It seems like a long wait, but it needn't be. If you're ready now, think what you'll be a month from now! Find a match or two in the meantime and work out the glitches.

Hopefully you are using the Supplement to Pure-Bred Dogs/American Kennel Gazette Events Calendar. It comes free of charge to those who subscribe to the *Gazette* and always includes blank entry forms.

Let's say you want a Saturday show in April. Turn to a Saturday April date that you have open. The first thing you notice is that the shows on that date are listed in alphabetical order by the state in which they will be held.

Decide how far you are willing to drive, and remember the drive back. Except for special events or crucial competitions, we now limit our driving, one way, to three hours; two and one half-hours looks better; two hours or less always wins my vote.

UNDERSTANDING A SHOW LISTING_____

Assuming you do as we do, you would first designate the shows in those areas within your reach. The sponsoring kennel club is listed next, above the exact location of the show. If a college or other building is mentioned, prepare for an inside show; fairgrounds or field, an outdoor show.

Next mentioned is the closing date for entries, the entry fee, the Superintendent's name, and any restrictions. The closing date is just that. Late entries are returned, and not always in time for you to realize you missed the entry date and need to cancel your trip. If you do not receive your entry verification by the Wednesday before the show, call the Superintendent to whom you mailed the entry and check your status. Their phone numbers are listed in your calendar. (A word of caution − enter early. These speedy mail services do not always deliver what they promise. Last minute entries often fail to make the deadline.) Often times shows, especially inside shows, will only accept a certain number of entries. This is what we refer to as a restriction. Any such limiting information appears in the listing.

Finally you see a list of the judging assignments. This gives you the opportunity to check your judge against your prepared notebooks in advance. To many veterans, this is the key information. Some will drive hundreds of miles to show to a judge who preferred their dogs in the past, but won't cross the street to show to others. We have never followed a judge in this pattern, but there are some so incompetent with our breed that we would not pay to hear their opinion.

Lynnedora selected a show just fifty miles away, under a judge who draws no adverse comment from kennel club members or from us. The show will be held outside. As a rule, an outside show is a better choice for a first point show. Extremely crowded indoor conditions, coupled with intensified and reverberating sound, can daunt even experienced animals, and experienced handlers for that matter.

ENTERING THE SHOW

"How do I enter Throck?"

By mail. And to accomplish that, you have two choices. The Superintendent's address and phone number are printed in the A.K.C. calendar supplement. If you do not have the blanks that come with the calendar, the Superintendent will furnish entry forms to you. (Once you spend money with a Superintendent, you will automatically receive premium lists for shows in your and surrounding areas.)

The premium list, in addition to including entry blanks, provides a fund of information such as: members of the kennel club and their areas of responsibility; special rules pertaining to the show; directions to the showground; and a list of nearby motels. You will also find a list of the judges and the prizes to be awarded — traditional prizes or special.

The Entry Form

Whether you use the blanks from the premium lists or from the calendar makes little difference. Those from the premium list have the heading filled out, identifying the show being entered. The entrant must fill in that information on the calendar blanks. Be sure you do. Most important, be absolutely sure you fill out everything correctly. If you make a mistake, it could cause disqualification, especially if you haven't allowed yourself enough time before the deadline.

What is not allowed is the use of a photocopy that only includes the front of the blank form. The reverse of the form contains an agreement and instructions. When the exhibitor enters, he does so under the terms of that agreement. If it is missing from the form you submit, your entry will be rejected.

Mail your entry form to the Superintendent well before closing date. Is there any mention of a maximum registration? If so, enter earlier still. If you are at a show under a certain Superintendent and short on time to enter a subsequent show under the same Superintendent, you may enter with his representatives at the show.

Confirmation

In theory, a week before the show an envelope with two documents comes back from the Superintendent. The first is a judging program. It tells you in which ring each judge and each breed are scheduled and at what time. For example, it may say Ring 3, Judge A.A. Smith. 9:00 A.M. — Spaniels, Clumber 2-5-1D-1B.

You must present Throck in Ring 3, at 9:00, to be judged by A.A. Smith. As competition, you will have four bitches, making a total of five. Should Throck beat the bitches, she then must compete against the winner of the two dogs for Best of Winners. At the same time, she will compete against one other dog and one other bitch, already Champions, for Best of Breed. (We shall review the whole sequence later.)

As it turned out, Throck lucked into competition. With the more populated breeds, finding competition is not usually a problem. To find enough animals for a major might be a problem, but not for competition.

The rare breed owners seldom trust to luck. Many call friends who own their breed and invite them to come and compete. Others watch *American Kennel Club Awards*, a monthly subscription magazine that lists every winner of every class, of every show. It also numbers and names the competition. If seven Clumbers competed at Western Reserve the previous year, one might reasonably presume some of those owners will return for the current year. We all know what can result from presumptions and assumptions, but that method often works.

Also in the envelope from the Superintendent should appear an entry confirmation containing information about Throck. Be sure to check each and every item for accuracy. It will also give you the class entered, along with your catalog number. The catalog number is the one you will wear on your left arm while showing.

"Does this little piece of paper mean we are official?"

It does — unless the information proves incorrect.

If something is wrong on the confirmation form, go to the show and arrive at the Superintendent's table at least one-half hour before the start of judging. If the error is theirs, you can have it corrected. If the error is yours, you can sometimes have it corrected.

TRAVELING

Choosing a Motel

We suggest you make reservations. Rooms fill quickly close to a dog show. You received a premium list; check it for motels that allow pets.

"There are lots of motels in that area, but they only list three."

It could be that only three accept pets because many animal owners can be crude, rude, and thoughtless on occasion.

Sometimes you can call other motels than those listed and make arrangements. It may be that the reason they are not listed is only because they do not have a working arrangement with the Superintendent or the kennel club.

Another hint — often, even if the motel generally refuses pets, the revelation that your animal has its own crate, coupled with your assurance she will not bark when unattended, can often work miracles. Deliver on your promise, for all of our sakes.

One last thing, though, before we leave this motel business. The next time you stay over, the shows may be at different sites and widely spread out. Unless you like hectic morning dashes, select the motel closest to the second day's show.

Traveling Equipment

"Didn't you once tell us that we would need extra equipment for shows?"

We might well have said that. What you will need will not be devastating to the bank account. The list of things you could add gets staggering. Canopies, exercise pens, stand dryers, and so on.

If you find you want or need all that stuff at some later date, select carefully. For now, you really need only small purchases such as rubber tie-downs, those flexible connectors with hooks at either end. You will find a million uses for them, from securing loads to connecting space blankets.

Another good purchase are space blankets, red on one side, silver on the other, with rings of rope around the edge. Great for shading cars, crates, and exercise pens. The red side up draws the heat; the silver side reflects it. They neatly refold into an easily stored square, and shed water too.

You have a cooler and a water jug already. Maybe even a folding crate would be useful. That's up to you, and is a convenience, not a necessity. The crate you have comes apart, with time and effort. Or you can carry it, assembled, from house to wagon to shade to wagon to motel room to wagon, to . . . If a car is your vehicle, you will have to disassemble and reassemble each time you move to a new location. All the assembling can be time-consuming and annoying, but hardly a terrible task.

If you can afford an additional folding crate, you will save yourself time and annoyance. It folds in seconds to make a three foot rectangle with a briefcase-like handle. The rectangles are not light as feathers, but most everyone can handle them.

Lynnedora, transports a medium size dog. Some Toy owners could carry two animals in a shoebox. Those who show the giants had better own collapsible crates or very large vans.

We use a four crate system now. Those who contemplate one day owning multiple animals may want to consider it. Each animal that lives with us (twenty give or take), has his or her own house crate, or den. We keep bench crates in the dog vehicles so that a trip to town, vet, or elsewhere is no hassle, and airline crates for long trips. To top it off, we carry folding crates to any show where we intend to stay over. The folders also serve for puppies after the first month. A substantial cash outlay, but it was spread over several years and never regretted.

As far as the best place to buy supplies and equipment, there is no one such place, but it is certainly not the supermarkets or pet shops. We buy many items from wholesale supply houses. They all advertise and send catalogs. Some of them send to exhibitors whose addresses appear in show catalogs. Compare for quality, price, minimum order, and shipping costs. Many accept a telephone charge against a major credit card.

As often as not, we buy supplies at the shows, where vendors' prices are usually very competitive with other sources. The larger the show is, quite naturally, the better the shopping. And shopping is all important. Do not grab the first item you see and regret it two booths later.

Probably it is best to buy the tie-downs at a variety or hardware store, and the crate and space blankets either at the show or from a wholesaler.

If the weather holds, or you do not care about reasonable comfort, you have everything you need for now. If the weather calls for rain and you prefer reasonable comfort, you do not have everything you need. Keep in mind also that the rain does not always follow the weatherman's forecast.

No matter what kind of condition you find yourself in, standing for ten hours — especially a wet and cold ten hours — strains the parameters of civilized behavior. For very little money you can furnish each family member with a common aluminum lawn chair that will feel sooooo good.

And if it does rain? Leave your rain gear at home and it will assuredly rain. Do you know how difficult it is to groom white dogs while the rain pours down and lightning cracks? Getting the animals clean and dry is half the battle. The journey to the rings, across a vast sea of mud and ground water, with fifty to eighty pounds in your arms, is the other half.

What a dog show is not, especially during rain and mud, is an Easter parade. Nor is the ring Fifth Avenue. Buy something that will keep you dry and warm. Too warm? Better too warm than too cold. Open the snaps of your coat. A hooded plastic jacket and rubber moccasins will get you started for about thirty dollars.

Transportation to the Show

It does not seem to matter whether the vehicle is a Volkswagen Bug or a block-long motor home, there is never enough room. With only one animal you can make almost any vehicle work. The choice becomes critical with multiple animals, a fact we shall elaborate on in Volume II.

Capacity, however, is not the only factor involved when considering vehicles. We also must think of mileage costs and overnight savings. Twenty-six cents a mile, the factored cost of operating a standard car, is a healthy enough bite. That three hour trip, say one hundred and fifty miles each way, winds up costing seventy-eight dollars in car expense alone.

Do not join the many who delude themselves about the costs. An entry fee still counts toward the cost of a show, even though you wrote the check the previous month. And it does cost more to eat out than to eat at home. Gas may well be the only out-of-pocket vehicle expense, until the repair bills and tire replacement charges arrive. And oh, the pain of a car trade-in!

A vehicle that requires a larger initial investment, expensive repair parts, and more gas per mile, only accelerates cost per show. Of course the motor home can save the motel expenses, and no one can argue the convenience of it on the showgrounds. Those who own them tell us we need only wield a pencil and paper to calculate the cost effectiveness. No argument here, but when we try those numbers, convenience gets very expensive.

Campers might consider vans. Some of the showgrounds offer showers and other facilities. Certainly a van is easier to buzz into town to a restaurant than is a motor home. But with a self-contained motor home, who needs the restaurant?

For the single animal owner, the compact station wagon probably offers the maximum convenience for the least cost. Agreed, overnight then includes a motel. But the motel bill is paid and goes away. Those vehicle payments go on and on and on.

After you make room for the priorities, fill the cracks and crevices of your vehicle with anything you desire. We assume you have a vehicle large enough for Throck to ride in her assembled crate. If not, purchase one of the special safety belts for dogs and let her ride with the family.

Everyone involved being in charge of certain items is helpful. For example, your son can be responsible for the photographic equipment and your daughter the tack box. It cannot hurt to fasten a checklist into the tack box. Those items often grow legs during the course of events and walk to other, less noticed areas. Run down that list and avoid those frenzied dashes to the vendor for items that should be there.

A second checklist may be helpful to avoid forgetting any of these necessary items. Why spoil an outing over a mistake that could be avoided. We all experience memory quirks. They increase with age.

The most important things to remember are that Throck needs to eat, drink water, and be safely restrained. Dry food is in a plastic container, and water in a jerry can. Food and water bowls are packed. The bench crate is in the vehicle, the folding crate for overnight we'll purchase at the show. Throck's jogging collar and the lead are in the house waiting for him and the show leads are in the tack box.

One last appeal to those who, for whatever reasons, take their animals to shows without crates. We appreciate your desire to see the entire show. For several reasons, we think most people should stay as long as they can. But for you, the amount of time you stay should equate with the amount of time you are willing to be out with your Throck on lead.

Please do not put your animal back in the vehicle after the competition and go your own way. Without a crate, the windows can only be cracked. The vehicle can overheat dramatically in a very short time. We are tired of seeing helpless animals panting and drooling, inches away from heatstroke. In fact, we are so tired of seeing this treatment, we think the A.K.C. representative should report any owner who allows his animal to suffer those conditions and that the organization should suspend their privileges.

Do not forget the vehicle check: fluid levels, lights, tire pressures. If not already in the vehicle, pack battery cables, flares, and a modest tool kit.

Undoubtedly space is getting scarce already. And you still have to add the people things. Clothes, rain gear, jackets, cooler, and the aluminum chairs. If any of the family requires special medication, pack it in a safe, accessible place.

When it comes time to pack, gather all of the items together first. Being able to see shapes and sizes will help promote efficient use of space. Once it works and you have everything in the vehicle, take time to make a little drawing of how you did it. You will be doing this again. There is no need to face a trauma every time.

Use your tie-downs to secure everything in the load. A quick stop to avoid a crazy driver can launch dangerous projectiles such as grooming tables. Do not risk fracturing someone's skull with flying debris.

Remember to allow yourself plenty of time to arrive before you show at nine. Arrive two hours early. Allow an hour for driving. Leave time to eat some breakfast.

Let us look at your list one more time. Forgot one of the most important things of all. A pooper scooper. Better add plastic bags with ties and an extra roll of paper towels also.

YOUR DOG'S CONDITION

Throck's stress will undoubtedly never reach the levels that anxiety does in you. To add to your anxiety, Throck's stress, in large part, depends on how you treat her.

Certainly the outing is disruptive, and in hot weather, even tiring. But she will still be up for meeting other dogs and playing with new people. She will want to have fun. See that she does, and see that you do too. This is not a life and death situation, or anything close to one. It's a sport, with very subjective judges, and many more losers than winners.

You know the secret; you came prepared. Throck is condition

ed and trained; you are conditioned, trained, and practiced. All you can do now is execute. The rest is out of your hands.

If Throck ever looks dragged out, or loses her enthusiasm, rest her. Rest yourselves. Too many shows too close together can burn out anyone.

You will hear people suggest supplements. There are almost as many suggestions as there are people suggesting vitamins, minerals, and home concoctions. Consult your vet before you use any. Two different animals, depending on their body chemistry, can extract different elements from the same compound.

We can offer a suggestion for those times when you are already out and your vet is not accessible. Go back to basics. Is she getting her accustomed exercise, play, and loving? Sometimes we get so busy at shows that we neglect the star. She's not above sadness, nor will she hesitate to punish you for ignoring her.

Is the temperature comfortable for her? Is she in season? Are there signs of illness? If she has every reason to be healthy, the weather is good, and she's not ill, then maybe she is tired. Make a canned food gravy and pour the increased fat over her dry food. If that doesn't pick her up, go home. The love relationship comes first. The athletic duo can challenge another day.

12.

Pre-competition Strategy

THE SHOWGROUNDS

When you step out of your car at the showgrounds, you will do so as a recognized exhibitor in a sport that has been a part of American life at least since May 1877, the date of the first Westminster Kennel Club Show. Next to the Kentucky Derby, dating from 1875, the Westminster is the oldest continuously held sporting event in the United States. Think what that event might be if the A.K.C. had the Derby's public relations people.

"Throck looks hungry and we look nervous."

You can feed Throck a small ration when we get there and give her a good drink. You should not give her anything before you leave on the trip. She is bathed, brushed, and beautiful, but getting sick while traveling could change all of that in a hurry. At her age, longer auto trips are better undertaken on an empty stomach.

Our experience rates car sickness at about one in ten dogs. Usually it happens a half a mile from the showgrounds when you are on a tight schedule. They grow out of it, as a rule.

Arriving at the Show

Again, leaving home early is important because directions to the showground are not always clear. Sometimes they are correct to the tenth of a mile, no matter from what direction you come. Others leave it to guess. In theory, as you draw near the show, you will note prominently displayed arrows labeled Dog Show, and pointing in the correct direction. Again, some clubs do a wonderful job, others do not. In foul weather, especially, a club representative should check those arrows every so often for rain and wind damage. How discouraging to a novice to drive two hundred miles through inclement weather only to miss competition because of poor directions and drowned arrows.

At the end of the arrows is the showground. The grounds do not always adjoin a highway. Often you must travel poorly marked, two-lane country roads for miles.

Frequently there are a lot of cars and people at the showground early. All the club members who volunteered to work had to arrive early, as did all the people who work for the Superintendent. The motor homes belong to exhibitors and owners. Most of them have been here all night.

Whether motor home owners or not, you can depend on the professional handlers arriving early. They are easy to find. They spread their crates, exercise pens, tables, and a great amount of other equipment over a large area, claiming a disproportionate share of the available space. Not all the professionals do so, mind you, but too many do. Living with that practice at outside shows is usually easier than at inside shows, but not always.

Now please remember, we have many friends in these ranks and admire what they do for the sport. At the same time, we cannot excuse or defend the faction that continually abuses the rights of others at the show and the rules of the show itself. A printed rule banning exercise pens in the building should pertain to all participating.

The professional will defend excesses by reminding us that this is his living, that the nonprofessionals are just playing. Bunk! If there are no nonprofessionals, there is no competition, and so no professionals. A peanut vendor makes his living at a ball game. We do not let him stand on the seat we paid for, or block our view because he makes his living there.

Many of the professionals are courteous and some extremely helpful. The only point we wish to make here is that there is nothing in the A.K.C. rules or show rules that says a professional is entitled to any more than anyone else who pays an entry fee.

Before we leave this soapbox, we should like to come down just as harshly on the breed clubs and nonprofessionals who follow the same practices. It is a word, too, for the kennel clubs who allow this. Manners and consideration should not be confined to the ring.

The large, commercial canopies are furnished by the Superintendent. He also supplies the ring dividers, ribbons, and catalogs. The catalogs will be sold by one of the club members acting as a parking attendant. He will assess a parking toll. Most clubs ask a dollar or two. He will also offer you a catalog.

You do not have to buy one every time, but certainly do so the first time you are at a show. They usually sell for around three dollars. That's a cheap price to see Throck's name appear in print.

Actually, a catalog can prove very helpful to the novice. In the front, you find a copy of the judging schedule. Then each and every participant is listed alphabetically by breed, by class, and by order of entry. The listing contains registration name, sire, dam, birthdate, breeder, and owner. It is fun to see it printed for the first time, or fifth, or tenth.

When you signed the contract, you agreed to keep our kennel name as a prefix in Throck's registered name. Thus she appears as Rose Run's Throckmortana. By looking at the breeder's name, you know who owns Rose Run. The owner's name tells who is exhibiting her. If an agent is listed, then you know the owner handed her off to a professional. When you breed Throckmortana, your kennel name will replace Rose Run as the prefix for the puppies.

The catalog offers an additional section of value. The names and addresses of all exhibitors are listed alphabetically in the back. Knowing where you can contact some of these people can often prove helpful.

For future reference, there is always a table under one of those canopies where they also sell catalogs. Sometimes you buy one just to see who your opposition will be.

The parking attendant will also show you where to park. Well, do not just take any place he gives you. Regardless of what that good gentleman may wish, you just paid to park. If that spot does not satisfy your needs, or threatens you in some way, wave him off, explain, and park elsewhere.

You certainly do not want to park in a pond or mud hole where your family, forced to operate in such an area all day, will be most uncomfortable. And if it rains, the tractor operator will charge twenty-five to thirty dollars to extricate you. Note that level ground is best for grooming tables and a shady area is best for crates.

THE SHOWGROUND LAYOUT

The Center Aisle

There is a rectangle on the level area that resembles the one you saw at the match. At this show we have a canopy-covered central aisle, with six rings off each side. Because of the length of the total rectangle, there is a second aisle, perpendicular to the central aisle, setting up three rings in each of the four sections. The rings were marked off with rope at the match, but these rings are divided by wooden fences set in the ground.

An inside show would be set up the same, without the canopy and quite likely, without perpendicular aisles. Depending on the surface of the floor, the areas are either entirely covered, or partially covered with rubber matting on which the animals compete. In either case, the surface is non-skid.

The National Anthem is played at the beginning of the show. The judging starts as soon as the music ends. There they go. Let the competition begin.

Judges' and Stewards' Table

Just as you found them at the match, the entrances to the rings all open off the central aisle. Near each of those entrances, just inside the ring, you find a table for the use of the judge and the steward, or stewards. This is the place you go to get the number that appears on your registration receipt of "Admit One," as we call it. That same number should appear in the catalog and is the number you will hang on your left arm.

You could get in now or at any time after the start of judging. That's a good job to assign to a helper. At every show, just have him give the steward your breed and number. And tell him to remember to get a rubber band or two from the bag hanging on the fence. Where he decides to put it until Mom is ready does not matter, as long as he puts it in the same place every time. You do not want to have to chase him down for the number.

Condition of the Showgrounds

He should also report the condition of the aisle to you. If it is wet and muddy, you will need to bring a space blanket and towel for Throck to lie on while she waits. If it is dry and firm there are two less items to lug around.

While the central aisle at an indoor show is, out of necessity, often reserved for — and restricted to — exhibitors with animals, at an outdoor show, although the necessity may still exist, anyone — spectators, exhibitors, helpers — can crowd that passageway. Rain makes matters worse.

As bad as it gets and though we complain, under the present conditions there is no desirable way to avoid it. We favor inclusion of the public, and urge all possible effort to increase that participation. The more interested viewers a show draws, the more we increase the numbers of fans and potential participants. In every area where a show is held, there are tens and hundreds of dog owners and lovers who have never seen a show. We find that hard to accept.

The kennel club, A.K.C., and show superintendents need to give more attention to accommodating the public. No wonder the center aisle is crowded. With connected rings, it provides one of the two views of a given ring. And if spectators do find a place where they can see, most watch in ignorance of what is happening until the group competition. Certainly no one gets on a loudspeaker and explains baseball to those who buy tickets, but baseball has millions of sophisticated fans who have been catered to and educated over the years. We dog fanciers complain about puppy mills, lab testing, and animal cruelty. At the same time we waste opportunities to reach, interest, and educate the public by clinging to an exclusivity more appropriate to the polo set.

Obedience Rings

In the larger rectangle that surrounds the rings, there are some other areas you should note. Please keep in mind that due to space limitations and irregular terrain, outside shows are not always neatly structured. The parts are always there, somewhere, but not always arranged in neat squares and rectangles. Notice that down off the far end of the rectangle there are four more connected rings.

"Obedience rings, I bet."

Exactly right. Many inside shows and some outside shows do not offer obedience because of space and facility limitations. If a large building is available, obedience is often held inside, even at an outside show. Otherwise, with only the rare exception, you will find the separation of conformation and obedience rings as you see them here.

The Grooming Area

There is a large canopy at the end, covering the grooming area. Nothing much to describe, it is a somewhat flat and dry area under a canopy, where people can groom their animals and be protected from rain. Sometimes electricity is available. Those with the animals requiring a lot of work make extensive use of this area, if they can find room. The space grabbers operate here, also. Those with Sporting dogs, Hounds and the like, usually forgo the grooming tent – in good weather at any rate – and groom near their vehicles.

An inside show often does not have this luxury. Some shows designate a space as the grooming area, but, more realistically, any nook or cranny outside the rings and traffic flow works well too.

Superintendent and A.K.C. Representatives

The smaller area, close to the grooming tent, serves as headquarters for the Superintendent and the A.K.C. representative. Problems with entries go to the Superintendent. Issues over show conduct, judge deportment, and A.K.C. rules infractions should come to the attention of the A.K.C. representative.

Actually, in all of our years of dog shows, we have only had one occasion to go to the Superintendent to bump an animal from class status to special status. That is easily accomplished, if you do it at least one-half hour before judging commences. Friends have gone to the Superintendent because of owner errors in registration, judge substitutions, or withdrawing a sick or injured animal. Reports that we hear complimented the courteous treatment. No money ever came back, but the refund was denied pleasantly. Only once did we ever seek out the A.K.C. representative. She openly admitted that they support the judge, unless there is flagrant error or abuse of rules. We lost (the judge said one thing and wrote another in his book), but we were well treated by the knowledgeable lady throughout.

Items for Sale

All those other canopies, of various shapes and colors, belong to vendors and company representatives. Food and supplement advocates, grooming and kennel supplies, art, crafts, books, and jewelry are all among the items you can buy. At a show this size, nearly three thousand animals, you should be able to find most anything that remotely relates to a dog.

GAINING AN EDGE

Let's take Throck for a walk. Ring three sounds like a good destination.

"Ring three, that's where I'm showing. I get the feeling we didn't walk Throck down here by accident."

Most decidedly not. This is called mixing business with business. While husband unpacks the grooming equipment, supervised by your daughter, the assistant groomer, you give Throck a chance to stretch her legs, investigate the new situation, and do her business.

This jaunt can prove very important to you. The primary objective is to get Throck to dump. Although it happens often, it really is poor form when an animal does it in the ring. At the same time, you can add to Throck's socialization. Walk her down the center aisle, weaving her through the crowd of dogs and people. She is with the pack leader, nothing can hurt her. Then walk around the outside of the rings to your ring. Check it out carefully: Small or large? Rectangle or square? Smooth or irregular terrain? Level or slanted?

If you have an animal that is prettier than it moves, hope for a ring with an uneven surface. That same ring penalizes the good mover. Plan your strategy now, ahead of time.

Watch the stacking of the dogs showing now. Is the area level, or are there dips and swells? Pick a spot you like, along with an alternate. Unless the judge requires catalog order, head for one or the other when you enter the ring. You do not want to disadvantage Throck by stacking her up or downhill.

Look at the patterns the judging is calling for. The judge will use the same one all day, if he can. Weather conditions or an unexpected hazard may force him to change patterns. You have a mental edge now. You know exactly what to expect from the judge. Close your eyes a moment and walk yourself through it.

Now watch the judge. What pleases him? He keeps looking to the animals with outlines most true to type. There are three of them in this ring now – first, second, and fifth position. The woman in fifth lost her stack. The judge smiled, but turned away. He has no patience for poorly trained animals or unpracticed handlers. The woman in second, because her animal is small, would have been better advised to move farther away from the large animal in first position. Her animal has the best head and balance, small or not. The handler knows it and is doing her best to assure that the judge gets the message. The judge wants to take a closer look. First position handler is busy smiling at ring-siders and does not see him. Oh, now he realizes the judge is nearing his area. He tries to think what he and his dog should be doing, but it is too late.

The animals are going around the ring now. The second animal is not the best foot dropper, but he has style. The judge took a close look at that head and liked it. The first animal's head is close, but the handler did nothing with it when he had the opportunity. The animal in fourth position moves like a cloud, with a great foot drop. That won't impress this judge. He came to evaluate beauty, not function. The second position animal wins.

From this preview you should know what to emphasize then you show the judge Throck. And you also know what to write in your notebook for the next time you meet this judge. Now you understand why you exercise Throck in this direction and wind up at your ring. Mix business with business. By doing so, you have a step up on your competition. The other exhibitors may do the same things and watch the competitions before theirs. Some will not know what they are seeing; others may misinterpret what they see. Some will understand just as you do. In this case, you won't have the advantage, but neither will they. Just hope you have the best animal.

"Are you saying the best animal always prevails?"

No, we cannot say that. We cannot even say that the best animal in the judge's opinion prevails. We can say that many times the animal that is, in the judge's opinion, the best on that particular day, wins. We may not understand his criteria, but we cannot overturn his decision. Do not waste time thinking about things you cannot alter. What is the job for you and Throck? Execution, plain and simple. The rest is out of your hands.

VIDEOTAPING SHOWS

Video equipment is a definite extra for most who are showing dogs. We understand that. But it does make things easier. Taping competitions gives you the opportunity later to look objectively at your performance. It also gives you other handlers — both good and bad — to compare yourself with. In case you decide to make the investment, here are some tips we have picked up along the way in using our video equipment.

First, of course, is the basic tool — the camera. From the beginning we want you to understand that improvements in the field of videography occur often, much like computers. What is here today may be obsolete tomorrow.

Although there appear to be several brands of video cameras on the market, our understanding is that two or three companies make them all. That should reduce the quality variables, item from item. What we need to look for, then, is the basic unit, with the most desirable options, for the least money.

Start with a VHS format camera that uses the same film as your VCR. The unit should have a power zoom lens 6:1 or 8:1, which assists you in focusing on items in motion.

As with your 35mm camera, there are several lens types available. You may want to add a wide angle and a telephoto lens, just as you did with your still camera. Be sure to ask about the focal distance of any lenses you purchase. They should not have more than a four inch focal length, or a four inch area in front of the camera within which the subject is too close to focus.

Check the lux rating. The lux number indicates the efficiency of the lens in conditions of low light. Seven works at twilight. The lower the number the more efficient at still lower light readings. Low lux is good; seven lux is decent; high lux is inadequate.

Shutter speed demands another consideration. The faster the shutter is recording the image, the less the blur is when the film plays back. 1/500th of a second is satisfactory. 1/1000th is better.

Do not overlook the automatic options. A charge coupler device electronically transfers image to film. This is a good option to purchase because it reduces glare and ghosts. An automatic focus does just that — handles the focusing for you. An automatic exposure makes sure subjects do not come out too dark or too light.

Buy the automatics if you can manually override and control them. The automatic focus, keep in mind, will focus on the nearest object. Without an override, you could wind up with great shots of the judge and poorly focused animals. We use the automatic to focus on the dog, then override to hold the focus there. Unfortunately, that only works until the judge moves the dogs. A similar problem arises with the automatic exposure. It locks on the subject and is not sophisticated enough to react to intense reflected light, such as that bounding off water and snow. You can override this weakness if you have the manual override option.

The available options, we feel certain, will continue to increase in quantity and improve in quality. We have two — a date stamper and a character generator. The latter allows us to add a caption with information about the show or animal to the film.

A tripod is a must purchase for the many times when you are shooting for hours from the same location.

Although we might enjoy having any number of the other options, the only other one that would appear to serve us often is the flying erase heads. This option eliminates those annoying static spots that appear between the stopping of taping one subject and taping restart.

If it comes down to a "this store or that store" situation, go with the one that offers the most comprehensive service contract for the least extra charge. Repairs and adjustments are often costly and often too frequent. Protect yourself.

Always try to keep an extra battery at hand, perhaps storing it in a plastic bag. A two hour capacity is good. You can buy one hour capacity batteries also. There is no particular savings of one battery over the other. The two hour costs about twice the one hour. The extra battery comes in handy, but is one of those items you can add as you go along.

Film, on the other hand, leaves you no option. Not only must you buy it, but it pays for you to purchase the best available, a brand designed for your camera.

We can understand that a video camera may be too expensive to buy right now. It took us a long time to afford one also. If we did not need it for business reasons, we might still not have it. But they do make things easier.

SHOWTIME IS NEARING

Showtime is nearing now. It's time to take Throck back and touch her up. On the way back we pass the food vendors. Perhaps the prices will actually be reasonable and not too outrageous today. There is a lot of competition so the capitalist system is in action.

As far as the quality of the food, what they cook at these shows can range from pure grease to decent. Experience teaches you where you usually find what. Once you have been to a show and come home with stomach cramps, or worse, record that in your show notebook. The next year you can pack sandwiches.

The show notebook is a very important record of the shows you attend. It is the one you keep alongside the judges' notebook. List the shows you have attended and all information pertaining to them. Things such as actual drive time, landmarks, sneaky turns, bad food, good accommodations, and so on. Anything that could make next year easier.

Throck is now back in her crate, the finishing touches placed on her grooming, and with an hour to spare before showtime. While it may seem premature to finish the grooming already, and there is a chance she could get messy again, take the risk. Do what you can, while you can. You never know what interruptions might present themselves before ring time.

If you can possibly make it work, do most of your time-consuming grooming at home. Trying to groom at the show intensifies the pressure on both human and animal. Ideally, leave only touch-up for the showgrounds. Have them so close to being ready for the ring that, in a pinch, you can dash madly from vehicle to ring as soon as you arrive. As memory serves, we did that more than once.

A snip here, a snip there, that missed hair, or grass and other various last minute stains — those are the touch-ups you make at shows. You have plenty of time, as a rule, for those. That way, when the young couple strolls past and asks for information on Clumbers, you will not feel threatened because you have too much to do. It is always better if the interested public waits to ask questions until after you show, but most of them do not know that. A few accommodating minutes can pay large dividends. Potential pet owners can be inspired to consider showing and those unsure of their breed choice can be wounded by the Clumber-cupid arrow. We cannot count all of the people who met us at shows and six months, a year, or even two years later purchased a puppy. Many are showing their animals as we speak.

Lining up customers is not of great importance for you at this moment. But it is important in the long run. If you intend to breed one day, a subject we discuss at length in the next volume, you must keep in mind that it takes several generations to make reproducible changes. Generations mean litters, litters mean puppies. As much as we would like to keep them all, most of us could not provide the space or afford the food and care. Thus, if the goal is to improve the breed, you must keep breeding. If you must keep breeding, you must sell puppies. If you must sell puppies, you must have customers.

Even if you decide against breeding, be a good breed spokesperson. Send those happy, informed, excited people to those who do breed.

13.

Showtime

"When should we start for the ring?"

You will want to be there ten or fifteen minutes ahead of time to let Throck adjust to noise and other white animals. During that time, park her a ring or so away, since you do not want the judge to assess her in the aisle when she is not at her show ring form. And watch her closely; do not let her annoy animals, handlers, or spectators, or let them annoy her. We can guarantee that the moment you get busy chatting and take your eye off her, she will get dirty, hurt, or in trouble. Socialize later. During those last few minutes, focus your concentration and hers; communicate with her. When you hit that entrance, be a team.

Please keep in mind that the focus of this work is preparing animal and owner/handler for competition in the conformation ring. On any given day, at any given location, any number of competitions can occur simultaneously. As a general rule, however, all-breed shows offer only conformation and obedience competition.

From many comes one. Thousands of animals enter a conformation competition, but only one emerges with the prize for Best in Show. The route to that lofty award sounds much more complicated than it is.

Let's go back to your entry. When you received a response from the show Superintendent, the enclosure contained a number, which is the number under which your animal will compete. It could be a small number, such as eight, or a larger number, such as 149. The superintendents issue the numbers in a system compatible with their record keeping. You need not concern yourself with the why and how. The only concern for you is that each dog you enter has a number of its own.

Before you will be allowed to compete your animal, you must go to the ring where you animal is assigned to compete and inform the steward of your breed. Lynnedora, for example, might well present herself to the steward and ask for the card issued to Clumber Spaniel - 6. The steward will hand her a cardboard number. Hanging in a bag near the steward are rubberbands. With the rubberbands, she must fasten the cardboard number to her upper left arm, with the number clearly displayed.

If Lynnedora had three Clumbers entered, she would request all three numbers and fasten all three to her arm, one over the other, with the number of the first dog in the ring on top. In like manner, if she entered three dogs of different breeds, she would go to each ring where she intended to compete and would again mount the numbers on her arm in order of appearance.

The time she is expected to present her animal at the ring is listed in the Judging Program. Assume that she checks the time and finds Clumbers are due at 9:00 A.M. She may also find that several breeds are expected at that ring at the same time and that Clumbers are near the bottom of the list, between Irish Setters and Cocker Spaniels. Judging will start at 9:00, following the order listed, the Clumbers following the Irish into the ring and preceding the Cockers. The steward will call each breed as soon as the judge requests them.

Once the Irish Setters have been judged, the steward will call for the first Clumber class. It is doubtful with a rare breed such as the Clumbers that all classes would be represented, but they could be. That would mean that there would be dogs and bitches entered in Puppy Class, Novice Class, Bred by Exhibitor Class, American Bred Class, and Open Class. In addition, there could also be existing Clumber champions competing, both dog and bitch. All will compete against each other for the right to be judged Best of Breed and represent Clumbers in the Sporting Group competition.

The steward first calls in Puppy dogs and the judge declares a winner of that class. Next would follow Novice dogs, Bred by Exhibitor dogs, American Bred dogs, and Open dogs. In each class, the judge selects a winner, which is usually a first place animal. If there are enough entrants in the class, the judge also awards second, third, and fourth.

A judge can withhold a ribbon in a particular class on the grounds that none of the contestants displayed sufficient merit. It seldom happens, though it probably should happen more often.

At present, many of the judges who employ this tactic unfortunately do so only as a means of drawing attention to themselves.

"Is there an advantage to be gained by entering one class or another?"

Sometimes. A Novice — too old for Puppy and too young for Open — might get a better look in the contest for Winners Bitch, where there can only be five contestants at most, than she would in the Open contest among twenty-five or so. A like advantage could accrue to any of the winners. Other than that, one tends to look on Bred-by and American Bred as arenas where the owners polish their own vanity.

Keeping puppies with puppies and adults with adults, however, should be — and theoretically is — important. The judge is supposed to calculate whether the puppy scores better as a puppy than the adult scores as an adult. On occasion, judging of that quality even happens. More often, though judges refuse to put up (this is the recognized term for advancing a dog to a higher level of competition) puppies, defending their positions by declaring the puppy may not retain his attributes and develop his potential into adulthood. The adult, on the other hand, is what it is. That logic relieves the judge from deciding whether the puppy is a better puppy than the adult is a better adult.

Almost as difficult to deal with, unless you own the animal, are the judges who fall in love with the cute puppy. Whether the puppy has merit or not becomes irrelevant. Cute carries the day.

When all of the dog classes have been judged, the first place winners from each class return and compete for the position of Winner's dog. Assume the Open dog wins this. The dog that took second place in the Open class then joins the remaining class winners in the ring to compete for Reserve Winner. Should the Winner's dog prove ineligible, due to error or fraud, the A.K.C. will belatedly declare the Reserve Winner to be Winner's dog.

Next come the bitches, and they go through the same competitions as covered above, Puppy through Open. Winner's bitch is selected, as well as a Reserve.

Still in the same ring, as part of the same competition, the steward now requests the existing Champions to enter the ring, and Winner's dog and bitch to join them. The judge must award a Best of Winner's ribbon to either Winner's dog or Winner's bitch. The judge will also compare Winner's dog to the existing Champions, called Specials, choosing from among them a Best of Breed and a Best of Opposite Sex to the Best of Breed. The Breed competition is over.

The Best of Breed animal is eligible to continue into the group competition. That takes place near the end of the day in a larger ring, possibly, but not necessarily, under the same judge. As you remember, the A.K.C. assigns all breeds to one of seven groups. The Best of Breed Clumber is entitled to compete with other Best of Breed animals for the Sporting Group against the other group winners for the ultimate award of the day — Best in Show.

POINTS

To backtrack a moment, all of the class dogs aspire to the right to be recognized as Champions. To accomplish that title, they must accumulate fifteen points, including two majors. Each major must be earned under a different judge and the total of fifteen points must be earned under no fewer than three judges.

Each show catalog and the *Gazette* carry a copy of the point values. The number of points awarded for defeating a given number of animals varies from breed to breed and geographical region to geographical region, factored by the A.K.C. according to the number of animals of that breed entered in the shows of that region the previous year. A Clumber owner in the East may only have to beat one other of its sex to gain a point. A Shepherd in California may have to beat seven of its sex for the same point.

Majors are awarded if an animal beats enough competition to qualify for three, four, or five points, five being the maximum number of points a class animal can win at a single show. Again numbers and regions are involved. The Clumber competing in New York may only have to defeat four of its sex for a three point major. The California Shepherd may have to defeat twenty for the same three points.

In the contest we just described, when all the classes were represented, only the Winner's dog and the Winner's bitch can win single points or majors. Suppose, for the moment, that the Winner's dog only defeated three other dogs and was thus only entitled to two points. The Winner's bitch, however, defeats seven bitches for a five point major.

When the dog and bitch contest each other for Best of Winners, the dog has much to gain and the bitch little to lose. If she beats the dog, it gains her nothing. If she loses to the dog, she loses nothing. The major is hers for beating seven other bitches, or the Class winners who in turn beat others. The dog, by way of contrast, if he beats the bitch, will also be entitled to a five point major for beating the bitch that beat the seven bitches.

The existing Champions, or Specials, can also win points for victories in these contests, but this additional complexity is more appropriately discussed in Volume II with our investigation of the Group and Best in Show contests. Those levels of competition require new formulas and new tactics and their own focus.

"What if we can't remember all that point business?"

Then you will have lots of company. Half of the veterans still have trouble with points. If you win and you are in doubt about what you won, wait a week and then call the A.K.C. They will explain what you have coming in points. If you wait a month, they will also verify that the points have been posted to Throck's account. The vast majority of the time you will find these amazing people have everything in perfect order. Just in case someone has a bad day, keep careful records of your wins — show, date, judge, and ribbons awarded.

OTHER TIPS

Enough on points! Let's take a quick look at some of the other aspects of the show. The people, for instance.

"They are all nicely dressed, I'll say that. With that many exhibitors, I expected to see a scruffy or two."

A scruffy or two would not shock us. Nor does their absence. The accepted practice, however, requires entrants to dress as the judge does. If he wears a tie and jacket, respond in kind. When the judge modifies his attire for rain, cold, or heat, that same latitude is allowed to you.

Certainly the occasion could arise where an accident renders your ring wardrobe unusable and you have to show in jeans, or whatever. The steward will not stop you at the gate. Neither, in all likelihood, will the judge penalize you. The eyes of those around you, though, may be troublesome; they will remind you to show more caution next time.

We should mention one last courtesy. It is permissible to show a bitch in heat in conformation. The judge will appreciate a warning during the exam, though. The judge may only ask the age of your animal. Nothing more!

Now walk with us to the corner ring. Cockers are competing there. Let's watch for a few minutes. Good, here is a hotly contested competition! You can learn some other things here. This one is down and dirty.

"Why? Is winning that important?"

Some of these handlers and owners think so. There are some nationally ranked animals and heavyweight handlers involved. The stakes are higher. This is the major league in the sport, so to speak. Without getting into detail (something we save for Volume II), it is the world of Group, Best in Show, and International winners, animals with national and international rankings and endorsement contracts. It is truly a different world. We mentioned that the Best of Opposite only wins a ribbon. When you campaign on this level, however, that ribbon means national points and a possible appearance in a nationwide advertisement − big bucks in other words.

On a day when you have time, study the grooming on the Cockers or Poodles. Leave hair there, take hair here, tease up, trim down, hide those cow hocks and stretch that neck. Interesting! Now watch these handlers. This one keeps a tight lead; stringing the dog up until his front feet hardly touch the ground certainly gives the judge a good look at natural gait. Watch that man stack his bitch on the table. He adjusts the head and front feet, gives a little downward push on the shoulders. That little push tends to lock the shoulders so the animal does not move its front while the handler adjusts the rear.

You have to look closely for dirty tricks. Number two handler stopped well in back of one to force three into that dip in the ground. Seven moved up on six so that six could not stretch his animal out. See how the top line is roached.

As they take them around, handler one slows to break two's stride, then speeds away. Seven runs up to the back of six, making six look like a poor mover. Five breaks momentarily because four tosses bait. There is lots of dirt in that ring.

"Is it a lot more difficult for Cocker owners to put a Championship on their dog than it is for the Clumber owner?"

The Cocker and other popular breed owners would love to have you believe that. A Clumber needs to defeat far fewer dogs on his way to a Championship than a Cocker, because there are far fewer Clumbers in the country than Cockers. On the other hand, a rare breed owner has to hunt and organize competition, sometimes traveling long distances.

We see a close correspondence to swimming. If you can skim across the surface, it does not really matter how much water is underneath. If the laws of genetics apply, the same percentage of great dogs will surface in the Clumber world as do in the Cocker world. On his way to a Championship, the great Cocker simply wades through more mediocrity than the Clumber.

VIOLATIONS AND DISQUALIFICATIONS____

"Why did the judge walk over to that spectator and make her move?"

Because he spotted a violation he could not pretend to ignore. The woman's husband is in the ring on the seventh bitch. The wife made noises to excite the animal and signaled her husband to make adjustments in the stack. They call that double handling, an example of unsportsmanlike behavior. This woman was obvious, but usually the participants strive to be subtle.

"What happens to the animal and handler now?"

In this instance, nothing. The judge suspected the violation and asked the woman to move. She promptly and quietly complied.

It would be unwise to give the judge a hard time. As it stands, he could disqualify the bitch from competition, in which case she no longer counts for points. If there were just enough bitches to make a major, the breed people would be very unhappy with the violator. Now, if either husband or wife became abusive, the judge could request A.K.C. to suspend his/her privileges.

There are several other ways to get disqualified. There are those that pertain to the animal's physical condition. Males and females must have all of their plumbing. That is to say, the males cannot be neutered or the females spayed. And nothing can be used to alter the natural color or texture of the coat such as dyes or chemicals. Neither can an animal be surgically altered for cosmetic reasons. Cesarean sections and life-saving surgery are allowed, of course, and other surgeries that relieve pain, but face lifts are out.

An animal can also be dismissed for lameness, which we understand and support. (If handlers spot the lameness well ahead of ring time, many fortify the animal with painkillers.) What we do not totally understand is the disqualification of deaf and blind dogs. Evidently blind and deaf aren't considered beautiful.

We have no reservations, when a judge dismisses an animal for aggressiveness. If an animal growls or snaps at a judge that animal should be dismissed. If we could only extend that rule to cover handlers who growl and snap. We have heard owners complain that the judge's heavy-handed tactics caused the dog's unusual behavior. This is possible. Heavy-handed judges do exist. A sickly dog, and a handler who mistreats a dog, will also be dismissed.

Then there are some technical things such as the animal that is registered in the wrong class or violates the standard in areas that require disqualification. That about covers it.

"Just in time. I only have twenty minutes and I still have to change."

Actually it will be about forty-five minutes. Look at your catalog again. Under your ring and time it lists Clumbers competing third, after several Setters and English Cockers. Those animals listed before you are, of course, judged before you, starting at the time mentioned. Though in this case it may take the judge a half an hour to get to Clumbers, it is impossible to say how long an average competition takes.

On days when you are running late, or for some reason such as inclement weather or illness want to get to the ring at the last moment, send a family member ahead to scout. When the judge calls the breed scheduled before you, it is time to head to the ring.

JUDGES

Who would we blame if there were no judges?

Many judges are excellent. They are involved dog people who

have handled and bred, study hard, and stay current. Many judges are poor. The contestant and his handler literally pay their money and take their chances.

Every judge goes through the same procedure to achieve that position. First they make application to the A.K.C., describing their handling and breeding experience. They must also satisfy the board that they have made other contributions to the sport.

The *Gazette* then notifies its readers of the application and invites both positive and negative responses. If there are no strenuous objections from the public, the applicant is granted a provisional license to judge.

A provisional judge must accept at least three assignments to judge the breeds for which he has made application and passed a written test. An A.K.C. representative will be present on each occasion to evaluate the provisional. Once this apprenticeship is completed the applicant becomes judge.

Unfortunately, all evaluations thereafter fall to the subjectivity of the judge. Worse, there is no accountability.

To offer an example of the impact a judge's subjectivity has on the sport, let us offer the following. With the same animal, we took first place at a National Specialty on Friday, fourth at an All Breed Show on Saturday, and first at All Breed on Sunday. In all three shows we competed against the same animals.

In defense of the judges, we must point out that the judge has only his eye and the soft language of the standard to rely on. These can account for some of the poor decisions, if not excuse them.

A judge is supposed to decide whether a puppy is a better puppy than an adult is an adult. That seldom happens. A judge is supposed to determine whether a Clumber is a better Clumber than a Setter is a good Setter, in terms of their standards. This seldom happens.

Judges do not even all agree on what winning signifies. Some will tell you that winning means your animal performed better than any of the other animals in the ring on that day. Style, showmanship, and presentation can count as much or more than the animal's actual appearance. Others insist that after evaluating a combination of traits − outline, bone and musculature, type, movement, etc. − your animal excelled overall. Some take that a step further. You are winner because your animal is the best prospect for breeding and carrying on the breed's traits. How would you like to be responsible for deciding that in two minutes?

Even gullible people like us have a little trouble with the grand myth. This one assures that judges only identify entrants by the numbers on the handler's armband, thus eliminating any chance of showing bias for a familiar animal or face.

Judges read the *Chronicle*, (a newspaper filled with full page advertisements extolling dogs being campaigned and their handlers), watch Bill Cosby and his handler interviewed on TV, attend other shows, and recognize P.H.A. pins as signifying a professional handler. In spite of all this, we are to believe they do not know when they are judging the top rated dogs and/or handlers in the country because they only refer to the numbers?

In reality, it does not matter if the judge recognizes special dogs and handlers that novices could pick out of the crowds. When a rookie pitcher takes the mound, the loudspeakers never hide the fact that Ted Williams, Hank Aaron, or the like is next at bat. If somebody else's Clumber becomes number one dog in the nation, we shall still show up to challenge. First, or one thousand and first, depend on us. And we won't even feel bad if we lose.

But if our animal does lose, we want it to be beaten by a superior animal, not an animal's superior publicity. That does not sit any better with us than showing to the judge who has had rare breeds simply tacked on his assignment and would not recognize a good Clumber if he stumbled over one. (Please remember, we keep referring to Clumbers because they are our 'for instance' dogs. Feel free to substitute any breed you show.)

Does it sound like we are overreacting? Probably! After all these years, we should be able to handle these little things without losing a beat. Why should we get bothered when our judge tells us ours is the first Clumber he has ever seen? Equally trivial is the judge who tells us there is a powder on the market that cures entropian (a turning in of the eyelashes that can only be corrected by surgery). Little things.

The good news is that a high percentage of the judges are honest, have a good knowledge of some breeds, and do the very best they know how. Most judges wouldn't fit the perfect portrait painted by some, but they would if they could.

And the news gets even better yet. A small change in the rules could provide an evaluation system that requires the judge to be accountable for his decision. As the situation stands at the moment, once a judge has judged, it is next to impossible to challenge any choices. Why? Because the judge does not have to commit himself beyond saying one, two, three, four.

The only place in the present structure where even a quasi-accountability appears is in the Group ring. Certainly no one could expect every breed winner from a given judge to place in Group. One here and there would do. A sprinkling of winners allows them to blame the losers or poor breed representation. But what happens if none of his choices ever place? Certainly someone from A.K.C. will ultimately ask the appropriate question. If not A.K.C. at least some of his peers will.

As a result, on far too many occasions, the judge selects an animal from Breed who will best compete in Group, the movement contest. These judges are not interested in the best representative of the breed because they do not believe the Group judge will evaluate each against its standard. The Clumber that wins Breed, then, is the one most capable of running with the Setters and Pointers.

A better way to make judges accountable would be to have them fill out rating sheets the way obedience judges do and hand a copy to the exhibitor. At least a verbal evaluation. We do not pay to learn our dog is better than another, nor to sponsor fault judges. We want to know why we win or lose. Would this be time consuming? Certainly! It would also be revealing, meaningful, informative, and value received for money paid. Let the stewards wield the pencils. Even a boxing judge has to keep a tote.

14.

Post-competition Strategy

We returned to the vehicle so that Lynnedora, Throck, and the family could enjoy the congratulations by themselves. Did they take Breed? With a bitch puppy? No, it was not a day of miracles. But she did take Best of Winners out of Puppy Class. That's bad.

"A major. I still can't believe it! Thank you for all your help."

Not us, thank yourselves. You all pitched in and worked as a team. It showed in the ring. The judge did not send the puppy to Group, but he treated her well. What does the family think about our sport now?

"They cannot wait until tomorrow. My husband is already talking about keeping a pup out of Throck's first litter. And the kids are pestering for more to do. They read something in the catalog about Junior Handling."

JUNIOR HANDLING

Junior Handling, or more correctly, Junior Showmanship, competitions are offered at every show. Many of the professional handlers came from those ranks. Junior Showmanship divides into four groups. There are Novice Juniors, ages ten to thirteen; Open Juniors, also ten to thirteen, but with three wins in Novice to their credit; Novice Seniors, ages thirteen to seventeen with fewer than three wins in Novice; and Open Seniors, thirteen to seventeen, with three wins in Novice.

Eight wins in the Open class — Junior or Senior — qualifies that person to enter the Limited Junior Showmanship class at Westminster, where the best Juniors compete for the very prestigious Leonard Brumby Senior Memorial Trophy.

The judges must be qualified to judge in at least one breed, and/or qualified to judge Junior Showmanship. Many of the judges are very considerate of and helpful to the contestants.

They realize that without a steady infusion of the young, the sport will soon die.

In Junior Handling, kids have to do the same things in the ring as adult handlers do, but the competition is different. Where your judge is supposed to evaluate only the dog, their judge grades only the handler. (Theoretically speaking, of course. Our observations tell us that the person on the best dog wins more often than not, in spite of the handler's quality.)

It is a wonderful experience. The children get to work with an animal, and compete against others their own age. It almost sounds too good and too easy. The one glitch for some people is that entrants must co-own or be of the family who owns the purebred. Children could work with the same dog that is competing in the regular competitions. It would be pretty tough on a puppy though, and confusing. Three contests every show.

An inexpensive pet is not the best idea either. With all fairness to the judge, it is very difficult to evaluate the child without considering the dog. Pretty well impossible. We think that the child with an outstanding dog will win more often than the child with a home boy.

If a show quality dog is available, though, the experience is wonderful for children.

HELPFUL HINTS

We stay for the end of a show as often as we can. A good share of the handlers arrive at the show at the last minute and leave the first minute they can. We never did understand that system. After competition, we talk with other owners and handlers and discuss outlook, technique, and animal illnesses. What a shame to waste such an opportunity. Talk, listen, sort, and add to your library of information. In the process, also add to your collection of friends. Unless you have a very long trip ahead of you to get home, try to stay for Groups and Best in Show.

Back to Groups. Stay if you can because hopefully one day, you will be a serious contender. Until then, watch the arena fill and bulge with professional handlers, owner-handlers, and gorgeous animals. Study the animals, scrutinize the handlers, cheer for your breed. Add and sift information, add and sift, add and sift. Soon you and Throck will be there, operating from your unique routine and information mix. When they hand you that first group ribbon, glance over and wink at the new crop of novices watching you.

New situations always provide opportunities for new problems, site problems, animal problems, and people problems. Be consistent in your approach to these areas. Get lax and it will catch up with you.

Then there is the question of surfaces — parking surface and ring surface. Rain and mud will be your worst enemies, followed almost equally by uneven terrain. Break, sprain, or strain something and you're on your own. The show organizers take no responsibility.

Ring size can complement or hamper your normal strategy. The small ring penalizes the mover; the larger ring penalizes the type and outline animal. The key word is penalize, not defeat. Develop an alternate plan for such occasions. Never get caught short.

You have rain gear, but you have never competed in it, or groomed in it. How will Throck react to rain? Your husband? The children? How will rain inhibit your routine? There are as many answers to these questions as there are animals, people, and situations. These answers each will have to discover for himself.

Cold weather brings inside shows. The noise increases, tempers shorten, and there is less room for everything. Loading and unloading often create the most tension. There is only one access way, two with luck, for 2000 cars. Arriving after the start of judging, if you can afford to do that, makes it easier to get to the door. You may not find a place to groom, but you will be inside.

With only one dog and equipment to worry about you will undoubtedly find it more convenient to park and haul your equipment in on a wheel base, or what we call a come-along, not to be confused with that used to tighten fence. A word of caution, the load will be top heavy. Watch for slopes, curbs, and holes. Do not let that load tip. Plan what you will haul ahead of time, and make sure it's not too much for you to handle on slopes.

There is also a type of indoor show called a benched show. They are few and Westminster is the most notable example. At a benched show you encounter all the unloading problems, but not the hunt for space. You are assigned space, enough for a bench crate per animal. (Check with the A.K.C. to obtain the allowable crate size for your breed.)

You must arrive before judging and literally bench your animal in its crate until the show closes for the day. You, or your representative, must remain near the crate to answer spectators' questions. These show are fun and different but make a very long day.

Some of the animal problems can be avoided and some have to be lived with. Car sickness, for example, can be avoided by withholding food for eight hours preceding the trip and slowing down for the dips and hills. Ironically, at the show the dog's other end becomes the focal point. Once the baby is fed, urge dumping through exercise. Fouling the ring can embarrass. Roaching and crabbing to avoid fouling up the ring can defeat.

Heat cycles for females must be lived with twice a year. Carry a can of room deodorizer for the vehicle and motel. Most of the male dogs you encounter will, hopefully, be on lead. Do not relax; a mating can succeed in seconds.

If it does happen, reprimand severely the dog's owner for not controlling his animal, then beat it to the vet for ECP. This drug, administered within twenty-four hours of the event, will prevent an unwanted litter of mixed puppies.

The other twice a year occurrence − the blown coat − though odorless, can easily be just as messy and ruinous to show plans. With the exception of a handful of breeds, dogs do shed. When they blow their coat, they shed a lot in a hurry. Grin and bear it. That's about all you can do. Some owners change food and shampoos to avoid it. They stuff the animal with supplements, but the coat still goes. (Do not be alarmed. When we say the coat blows, we do not mean the dog then stands bald before the world. That beautiful, glistening, textured, thick coat, however, will thin, thin, thin.)

Of course the coat comes back, eventually, assuming proper care and diet. It appears, though we would be hard pressed to prove it, that those animals who spend more time outside, in natural light, retain more coat than those who spend most of their time inside, in heat and artificial light. The fault in the observation is that most of our usually-in-the-house troops are the older dogs. Age could well distort the result.

Perhaps the worst animal problem is stress, leading to burn-out. Often times the stress is self-imposed as a result of being ignored. Keep Throck as close to routine as possible. Leave time in the show day for exercise, play, and plenty of affection.

Through the years, we found people-problems usually grew as large as you allowed them to grow. Remember that most of the people at the show are as excited and nervous as you are, including judges, stewards, owners, handlers, and spectators. When relations get strained, try a dose of understanding chased with compassion. Before you stiffen your back, walk in the other person's shoes. For good measure, add one more helping of understanding and compassion.

That is not to say that you should always back down, or ever back down, when principles and rules are concerned. On the other hand, being right for the sake of being right is not always necessary either. Project the outcome. If it "don't mean nothin'," walk away.

Some professional handlers can annoy you. (Interesting enough, the more experienced and capable they are, the less intrusive they are — give or take a few.) Some act as though they own the grounds, the judges, and the sport. They may never have owned or bred a dog and would flunk a canine anatomy exam, but they will fake expertise where it's lacking.

Those who are all show and no go are not limited to the ranks of the professionals. Look around. There are plenty of nonprofessionals who drive the same wagon.

You need only remember two things. If you paid your entry, there is no one who deserves more space per animal, more consideration, or more courtesy than you deserve. If someone takes advantage and acts as though he is entitled to special privileges, he will succeed only to the extent you allow him to succeed.

If you dislike a judge, refuse to show to him again. If you have good reason to question a judge's competence — if your opposition transcends personal dislike — urge your friends and kennel club members to boycott. No noise, no ceremony. Just quietly boycott. Now, if your disapproval stems from your conviction that the judge is political or otherwise dishonest, send your evidence to the A.K.C.

Rumor and innuendo often make things sound more hopeless than they are. Be careful! Do not give way to the myths. We often hear, for example, that you cannot win big in certain breed rings — Poodle, Shepherd, and others — unless your animal is handled by a politically connected professional. Now if that is not a myth, happily championed by the pros, then A.K.C. is asleep on its feet.

The fact that pros usually win in these rings is more likely attributed to the excellent dogs they recruit. That, and the fact that all those who believe the myth send them their best animals to handle. How often do the pros lose the Pro-Am golf tournaments? If proficient owner-handlers with superb specimens challenged time and again without victory, we might begin to wonder, but we shall never know until they try.

One more time, before leaving the judges, we want to remind you that you paid for an evaluation of your animal when you paid your entry. Placement is not an evaluation. How are they evaluating? Certainly they can't learn enough from their hands-on routine to substantiate an evaluation. Until we institute a system that holds the judges accountable for their decisions, we must continue as a sport subject to whim.

Most of all, be wary of the breed people: judges, pro handlers, and breeders. The nonprofessionals can cause as much stress as anyone, and there are a lot more of them. They come in several varieties. Those who do not know, and understand that; those who do not know, and think they do; those who do know; those who do know, and wish they did not. They are a microcosm of the world at large.

In dealing with this group, you have the advantage of being one of them. Even before you learn their name, you know you have a common interest and a bond. That's right — dogs! Make the most of it.

Finally, we must consider the general public. Be gracious. Build their enthusiasm for dogs and the sport. Tell them to come back often and bring friends. When we win Westminster with a Clumber, we want to hear the applause of fifty thousand people.

Just because the show is over for the day leaving does not mean your work is finished. Go out and have a good dinner, enjoy new friends, and get back early. Throck will need exercise, play, and affection, no matter the hour or weather.

Before the lights go out and while all is fresh in your memory, complete your show notebook. Record your actual costs for the day. Record show, judge, and ribbon data, along with your distance and conditions data on the show. List the motel and your impressions.

Then, do the judges notebook next. Be objective. Simply because you got the ribbon does not necessarily mean he is an exceptionally capable man. Consider what the losers thought of him. Better yet, ask them.

Review the whole day with the family, search for things that could be done better. Listen for problems, however small. The pack leader takes care of all it members. If any reorganizations are required, work them out so that they can be implemented in the morning. Packing, routine, competition, learning, pleasure — touch all the bases. If you do not show until afternoon, perhaps you can schedule a side trip to a point of interest in the morning.

"When will we see you again?"

When you want to take Throck to Group, Best in Show, International competitions or when you start having thoughts about breeding her. That time will be several memories down the road, but it will come. When it does, open Volume II. You will find us on page one, waiting.

Appendix I

GLOSSARY OF DOG SHOW TERMS

Angulation. Usually refers to angle at which bones meet at the joint in hip, the stifle to hock configuration.

Arm Band. Cardboard number displayed on left arm during competition.

Bait. Anything used to gain favorable response from dog. Ranges from food to toys.

Balance. Symmetrical proportions.

Backskull. Back of head.

Benched Show. Animals are displayed on benches for entire show.

Bite. Relationship of upper to lower teeth.

Chalking. Use of any foreign substance to alter dog's natural color.

Cheek. Part of head below eye and behind mouth.

Close behind. Hocks are close together when moving.

Close coupled. Too little length of back from last rib to hip.

Cobby. Too short-bodied.

Cow-hocked. Hocks turn toward each other when moving, while feet turn out.

Crabbing. Moves with rear feet outside front feet, or at angle with straight line.

Croup. The last part of the back before the tail.

Double Handling. A person known to the dog positions himself outside the ring and helps handler keep animal up, on the jazz.

Down in Pastern. Weak front ankles.

Drive. Action of rear legs pushing dog forward.

Elbow. Joint between lower and upper front arms.

Elbowing Out. Elbows turn out as dog moves, rather than staying close to sides.

Expression. A look that implies intelligence.

Fault. A defect in terms of breed standard.

Feathering. The fringe on ears, tail, and legs.

Finished. Animal has amassed enough points and major to claim Championship.

Flews. Overlapping lips.

Furnishing. See *Feathering.*

Gait. The animal's natural pattern of moving comfortably.

Gay Tail. Tail carried above back line.

Hackney. A high, affected-looking front reach. Overdone.

Haw. A third lid on inside of eye.

Height. Always measured from withers to ground.

Hocks. Rear ankle.

Layback. Angle of front shoulder in relation to forearm.

Leather. The exterior ear.

Leggy. Legs are too long.

Level Bite. Upper and lower teeth meet exactly.

Loin. Area from last rib to rump.

Low-set. Ears on side of head and/or tail attached below back line.

Occiput. Most raised portion of backskull.

Overshot. Upper teeth far overlapping lower teeth in front.

Pacing. Both legs on a side move at same time in the same direction.

Paddling. Forelegs do not provide proper lift.

Pastern. Joint between ulna and radius.

Reach. The amount of forward stride by the forelegs.

Rib Spring. Full, rounded rib presentation as opposed to slab sides.

Scissors Bite. Upper teeth overlapping, but still showing lower teeth in front.

Sound. A well structured, smooth moving, healthy animal.

Special. An animal competing in Best of Breed that has already completed its Championship.

Stacking. Posing the animal to present a balanced outline.

Sternum. Chest.

Steward. A person appointed to assist the judge in the ring.

Stifle. The rear knee.

Stop. A distinct step from nose to head.

String Up. Pose and/or move dog on tight lead. (To lift dog's front.)

Swayback. A back that sags in the middle.

Topline. The back.

Tuck Up. Belly slopes up to loin.

Typey. Very close to proper look of breed as described in standard.

Undershot. Lower teeth overlap upper teeth in front.

Withers. Highest part of body found just behind the neck.

Appendix II

BREEDS RECOGNIZED BY THE AMERICAN KENNEL CLUB

Sporting Group
Brittanys
Pointers
Pointers (German Shorthaired)
Pointers (German Wirehaired
Retrievers (Chesapeake Bay)
Retrievers (Curly-Coated)
Retrievers (Flat-Coated)
Retrievers (Golden)
Retrievers (Labrador)
Setters (English)
Setters (Gordon)
Setters (Irish)
Spaniels (American Water)
Spaniels (Clumber)
Spaniels (Cocker)
Spaniels (English Cocker)
Spaniels (English Springer)
Spaniels (Field)
Spaniels (Irish Water)
Spaniels (Sussex)
Spaniels (Welsh Springer)
Vizslas
Weimaraners
Wirehaired Pointing Griffons

Hound Group
Afghan Hounds
Basenjis
Basset Hounds
Beagles
Black and Tan Coonhounds
Bloodhounds
Borzois
Dachshunds
Foxhounds (American)
Foxhounds (English)

Greyhounds
Harriers
Ibizan Hounds
Irish Wolfhounds
Norwegian Elkhounds
Otterhounds
Pharaoh Hounds
Rhodesian Ridgebacks
Salukis
Scottish Deerhounds
Whippets

Toy Group
Affenpinschers
Brussels Griffons
Chihuahuas
English Toy Spaniels
Italian Greyhounds
Japanese Chin
Maltese
Miniature Pinschers
Papillons
Pekingese
Pomeranians
Pugs
Shih Tzu
Silky Terriers
Yorkshire Terriers

Non-Sporting Group
Bichons Frises
Boston Terriers
Bulldogs
Chow Chow
Dalmatians
Finnish Spitz
French Bulldogs

Keeshonden
Lhasa Apsos
Poodles
Schipperkes
Tibetan Spaniels
Tibetan Terriers

Herding Group

Australian Cattle Dogs
Bearded Collies
Belgian Malinois
Belgian Sheepdogs
Belgian Tervuren
Bouviers des Flandres
Briards
Collies
German Shepherd Dogs
Old English Sheepdogs
Pulik
Shetland Sheepdogs
Welsh Corgis (Cardigan)
Welsh Corgis (Pembroke)

Working Group

Akitas
Alaskan Malamutes
Bernese Mountain Dogs
Boxers
Bullmastiffs
Doberman Pinschers
Giant Schnauzers
Great Danes
Great Pyrenees
Komondorok
Kuvaszok

Mastiffs
Newfoundlands
Portuguese Water Dogs
Rottweilers
St. Bernards
Samoyeds
Siberian Huskies
Standard Schnauzers

Terrier Group

Airedale
American Staffordshire Terriers
Australian Terriers
Bedlington Terriers
Border Terriers
Bull Terriers
Cairn Terriers
Dandie Dinmont Terriers
Fox Terriers (Smooth)
Fox Terriers (Wire)
Irish Terriers
Kerry Blue Terriers
Lakeland Terriers
Manchester Terriers
Miniature Schnauzers
Norfolk Terriers
Norwich Terriers
Scottish Terriers
Sealyham Terriers
Skye Terriers
Soft-coated Wheaten Terriers
Staffordshire Bull Terriers
Welsh Terriers
West Highland White Terriers

Index